GW00373951

introduction

For a long time the UK's second city had little more than tower blocks, Spaghetti Junction and Nigel Kennedy. We've still got all that, but with the explosion of bars across the city, multi-million pound redevelopments and more shops than you can shake Ozzy Osbourne's headless chicken at, Brum is finally getting the nightlife and respect it deserves. Whether you're here for a night or you've lived here all your life, tuck into a flavour of the best and worst this fine city has to offer.

© itchy Ltd
Globe Quay
Globe Road
Leeds
LS11 5QG
t: 0113 246 0440 f: 0113 246 0550
e: all@itchymedia.co.uk
www.itchycity.co.uk

ISBN 1-903753-08-2

City Manager: Mike Waugh Editorial Team: Simon Gray, John Emmerson, Ruby Quince, Mike Waugh, Andrew Wood Design: Matt Wood
Cover Design: artscience.net Maps: Steve Cox at Crumb Eye Design
Contributors: John Herbert, Peter Sharman, Simon McQueen
Acknowledgements: Mat Alford, Jayne and Thomas Court, Helen, Cathleen and Alan Davis, Caroline Hunt, Ed Scully, Mat Ford, Dan Harrison, Richard Wilkinson
Jamie Oliver pictures copyright David Loftus

THE ONLY LINE UP THAT CUTS IT.
EVERY WEEKEND ACROSS THE GALAXY NETWORK.

BOY GEORGE
ALLISTER WHITEHEAD
PAUL OAKENFOLD   PAUL KERSHAW
                 KC-FLAVA ZONE
                 JUSTIN WILKES-CLUB TASTY

 Galaxy 102·2

contents

foreword

Jamie Oliver

These itchy guides are fantastic. When it comes to travelling, be it social or business, there's so little time to decide where to go and what to do. I spend half my life darting around all over the place, so when I'm visiting cities that I've never been to before, I like to cut to the chase and get to the right places. The itchy guides are just what I've been looking for.

These guides will definitely help you get the most out of a trip to a new city, and whether it's a two hour visit, a night on the town or a long weekend, the itchy team will push you in the right direction. From where you can find the most cutting-edge R'n'B to the coolest threads, as well as some good grub, a few drinks and maybe have a bit of a boogie. And at long last, someone's cottoned on to the fact that once in a while a dodgy pub and a bit of karaoke, beats posing at the latest bar opening, hands down.

It's reassuring to know that the itchy team take their research seriously. I know from experience that they certainly know how to mix business with pleasure.

– Jamie Oliver

For what's happening right here, right now and in 17 other cities... www.itchycity.co.uk. All the events, all the time, with news on gigs, cinema, restaurants, clubs and more. You can sign up for updates on anything from hip hop to happy hours, vent your anger about our reviews and get discounts for your favourite venues. Whatever's happening in the city, itchycity's there.

And for when you're out, we've made that hulking great big wap-phone actually useful. Next time it's 1am and you're gasping for a Guinness, whip out the wap and find your nearest late bar... **wap.itchycity.co.uk**

itchycity.co.uk

introduction

Let's face it, Birmingham gets a lot of stick, thought of nationwide as a grimy city of tower blocks and daft accents. Roit ah kid, 'taz soom trawth eenat, but times are a changing, and the redevelopment of Birmingham is finally taking shape. There's the sparkling Brindleyplace, an explosion of bars around Hurst Street, a growing scene at St Pauls, not to mention the Millennium Point, canal-side apartments galore and a whole host of work in progress at the Bull Ring. But the finest recommendation we can give is that Jeremy Clarkson hates the place. Bring it on...

We've focused on seven main areas:
City:
Aston Triangle: Of what there is, we've covered it
Broad Street: including Brindleyplace and Gas Street
Central: broadly covering everywhere from Millennium Square down to Digbeth and Hurst Street

St Pauls: Hockley, part of the Jewellery Quarter
Outside the city
Harborne: Suburbia for the 20 to 30s with an impressive selection of pubs.
Moseley: The bohemian part, where everyone refuses point blank to wear suits no matter what the occasion.
Selly Oak: Home to hordes of students from Birmingham University

Two hours

If you've only got two hours in the city centre, first ask yourself why you're not staying for longer, then leg it down to **Hurst Street** for some quality bar action in the **Arcadian centre**. You're pretty much spoilt for choice with a number of bars all huddled together, with **52 Degrees North** being the jewel in the crown. There's a whole pile of restaurants round here too, set right in the middle of the **Chinese Quarter**, but if push comes to shove, **Tepenyaki Restaurant** is the finest in the area.

If you're after a few earthy drinks your best bet is to head down to **Broad Street** where you're absolutely spoilt for choice. Almost all of the bars along here serve food, or you can stroll down to **Brindleyplace** for some riverside eating on a fine day. For a traditional pub, give the **Tap & Spile** a whirl, or for a more lively atmosphere, get down to the **Sports Café.**

www.itchybirmingham.co.uk

If you're after some quality shopping, you're spoilt for choice. Designer shops abound, and most of them should be open by the time you're reading this at **Mailbox** – just a short hop from New Street station. High street stores galore in **Pavilions** aren't too far away, but if you're really pushed for time, you should find something you like in the **Pallisades** which adjoins New Street.

Two days

Now this is more like it. For accommodation, you can spend as much or as little as you like. For luxurious high-rise lofty splendour, try the **Hyatt** right in the thick of the action on Broad Street, but if you're saving a few quid, get down to any one of the B&Bs in **Selly Oak**.

Sorted? Now take your pick from the cream of entertainments in the city.

Debauchery

If you're on a mission (and who isn't?), it's only fair to stop at a few pubs to get your drinking head on first. I Iam sees the first ones opening – try the **Factotum & Firkin** or **Newt & Cucumber** for a few sharpeners, both in the centre of town.

Slightly staggering, you can now lurch into a few bars down Broad Street. **Key Largo** have happy hours 'til 6pm every day but if

that doesn't grab you, there should be somewhere round here that does. Once the mish-mash of cocktails has shaken you up, you may want to stay up here all night (most of these places have a 2am licence), or head down to **St Paul's** for a more mature drink, or **Hurst Street** for a more laid-back one.

For the big night ahead, you've got a splendid choice of club action. House fans will find their nirvana at **Code** or the **Sanctuary**, whereas Nirvana fans will find their house at the **Academy**. Check itchybirmingham.co.uk for details. Cheesy pissed-up anthems move around the city, but suffice to say that **Zanzibar** do a pretty good line in the 'don't care about the music, just want to fall about' kind of nights.

Recovery

Feeling a bit groggy, shopping is always an option (see Two hours), or maybe a walk down by the canal on Broad Street. The **Jewellery Quarter** around St Paul's Church is worth a visit too. If you really want a full-scale fresh air country-side head-clearing recovery, take a short drive to the **Lickey Hills**, where a brisk 1/2-hour walk around beautiful countryside will see the most stinging of hangovers disappear. Those culturally inclined might fancy a trip round the **Ikon Gallery** or **Barber Institute**. Or if something a little less taxing is in order, **Star City** has 30 screens to keep you busy. Sports-wise, you could head down to **Villa Park**, though you're better off at **St Andrews** to watch the Blues. Cricket fans should have something to smile about too at Warwickshire's grounds in **Edgbaston**.

bars

www.itchycity.co.uk

Bar 2 Sixty

260 Broad Street (0121) 633 4260

In theory it's a great idea – take all the elements of a club and mix them up into one big bar, add a 2am licence and shake it up until fully cooked. But then you start thinking, why here and not one of the city's better clubs? Décor by numbers – long bar, pine, chrome, lots of seating and even a mini beer garden, but this place has got its aim set on a club vibe, and completely misses. Particularly crap is the idea that if there are only five people inside the place you should crank up the volume to ear-splitting levels in the hope they might start shimmying round the dance floor, maybe drawing in a few more punters. No, we'll just leave instead.

Mon-Sat 12-2 (except Tue 12-11), Sun 12-12. Fri/Sat £1 entrance 'til 10, £3 after. Sun £3 after 9.30pm

HH: Sun-Thu all day, Fri/Sat 'til 7pm selected 2-4-1 & £1 drinks

£9 Large steaks

Brannigans

196-209 Broad Street
(0121) 616 1888

These places vary wildly across the country, and although Birmingham is

FEEL THE P/RE.S/ENCE

JOSETTE SIMON. ACTOR.

A MELLOW MIX OF SPIRIT AND SOUL.
THAT FLAVOURS WHATEVER IT TOUCHES.

blessed with one of the bigger and better ones, you won't necessarily be jumping in a cab to get here. Everyone here is dripping in three-carat gold and luscious bright orange tans – except on Tuesday's student night which does a respectable pint of Vodka Redbull for £4. Think Yates's but a bit more clubby and you've just about got it – along with the clap should you ever choose to pull here.

Mon-Sat 12-1, Sun 6-10.30. £7.95 buffets Drinks promos Tue-Thu and $^1/_2$ price drinks Sunday.

Casa

Brindleyplace, Broad Street (0121) 633 3049

One of Broad Street's newest and best. Minimalist elegance without being stark or intimidating, this is an attractive, airy, chilled out bar. There are beautiful people here too but with no doormen and no dress code it's not the sort of place that'll turn you away for not sporting the right labels. Like a mini 52 Degrees, only quite a lot brighter and not quite as busy or exclusive. The raised restaurant is recommended, and in particular the Aberdeen Angus Steak.

Mon-Sat 11-11, Sun 10.30. HH: 5-7 every day

£7.95 Chicken special

Gio's

Paradise Circus (0121) 233 1891

Recently refurbed from the old Grapevine, you wouldn't recognise the place now a team of bar stylists have had their hands on it. Minimalist spotlighting, together with lashings of metal, blue décor and a more 'fancy' clientele relax in this wee L-shaped bar. Fairly unobjectionable venue, used by most as a meeting place before launching into a night of debauchery in Broad Street.

Mon-Sat 11-11, Sun 11-10.30pm

Grosvenor Casino Bar

Broad Street (0121) 631 2414

Big, bright and shiny bar with a strict 'smart and sharp' dress code and membership is essential. Good house and garage with resident DJs on Thursday, Friday and Saturday make this one of the more popular pre-club bars around. Huge seating space and a fair range in cocktails and shots. And most importantly, it's a warm-up for the casino upstairs to show everyone your ineptitude and naivety as a gambler when you try and put 50p stakes on evens.

Members only. Mon-Sat 4-2am, Sun 4-10.30. HH: 7-10 daily, all bottles $^1/_2$ price

£9.50 Scottish sirloin steak

Key Largo

193-194 Broad Street
(0121) 616 1300

Easy meeting place – "I'll see you by the two 8-foot metal lizards and flame-spurting torches on Broad Street". And inside, though it's not quite so mind-bendingly different, it does hit the spot. Bright and colourful with a sense of warmth during

the day and party crowd at night. Business schmoozers can usually be seen here during the week with some impressive penny-pinching drinks discounts, but then come the weekend, prices revert back to the usual Broad Street standards and the tunes crank up to club-level volumes. Usually food in bars like this is cooked by a bunch of cack-handed gibbons with spatulas; happily, the good folk from Celebrity Balti are responsible for the grub here, so it's some of the best around. Mon-Sat 12-2am, Sun 5-10.30. Fri/Sat £2 after 10, £3 after 11

£5 Balti plus naan. HH: all day 'til 6pm

Mellow / Stoodies

192 Broad Street (0121) 643 5100

All part of the same complex, but not the same kind of places. Mellow is exactly that – in amongst the bedlam of chaos on Broad Street, this is that rarest of venues where you can chill out in swanky settings, compared to the more gaudy and lively Stoodies at the back. Stoodies is only ever as good as the crowd it pulls in, and sorry to sound vague, that varies so widely on the night it's impossible to say. At its best it's a raucous night of up-for-it tunes with a happy and bouncing crowd, and at worse it's full of Gareth Cheeseman and friends reminiscing over great Kirby Vacuum sales.
Mon/Tue 10-7, Wed 10-2 (1am Mellow), Thu-Sat both places open 10-2am, Sun 10-10.30pm. Cover charge at Stoodies £3 after 10.30pm

£14.95 3-course turkey dinner

Merchant Stores

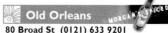

Broad Street (0121) 633 4207

It's a kind of wine bar. WINE BAR I SAID! Blimey it's loud in here – and that's really all you can remember. For lip-readers and those totally devoid of conversation, perfect. But it's only open 'til 11, by which time you realise that yes, it's too late to get into anywhere else, and no you haven't had a good night, and oh knackers, you've developed a lifetime of tinnitus to tell your grandchildren about.
Mon-Sat 10-11, Sun 11-10.30

£5 Rib-eye steaks

Old Orleans

80 Broad St (0121) 633 9201

This place shares as much with the deep South as Dudley with Paris. Usual big chain theme-heavy guff, with lots of 'authentic' crud adorning the walls, bright lights and an inordinate number of references to jazz and folk artistes that frankly

Name, age and occupation?
Lola, 27, architect

Nice C&A pose. Where do you drink?
RSVP and 52 Degrees. Though I like Arca.

Where's good for food? I love Petit
Blanc, but also a good balti does the job

And for clubbing? I don't

Sassy dresser? I like the new line at Reiss

Best thing about Brum? It's getting better all the time

Worst? The traffic wracks my nerves

wouldn't be seen dead in a place like this. A bit like TGI's in a Tex-Mex way, except there's a bar that's a venue in it's own right. But why oh why?
Mon-Sun 11-11pm
HH: 3-7 Mon-Fri selection of cocktails
£10.65 Ribs

Pitstop

**The Waters Edge, Brindleyplace
(0121) 644 5981**
Yeah so this was one of the first upmarket bars in Birmingham, but so what?. The bouncers expect you to be arse-kissingly grateful that they've let you into this shoddy effort in Brindleyplace and now there are so many other options, take

your hard-earned elsewhere. Location wise, it's perfect for drowning your sorrows – just take a running jump into the canal at the end of the night. The only time when this doesn't apply is Bar 125 on Thursdays when everything costs just £1.25, and a handful of reasonable people make it just about worthwhile.
12-11, Sun 12-10.30pm
**HH: 5-8pm everyday, Bar 125 Thu eve.
£4.75 Lasagne**

Ronnie Scotts

Broad Street (0121) 643 4525
This bar used to be a pre-club place with raucous tunes and a fully up-for-it atmosphere. They've refurbed and by 'eck, they've had a change of heart. Still good, but now in a completely laid-back, big chairs, "Shush, people are eating" older crowd kind of way. Sits somewhere between a bar and a restaurant, and not particularly big, or rather, 'intimate'. It's probably more in keeping now with the clientele who go on to the jazz club round the back, and although it's a shame to see the bar disappear, there are so many other alternatives on Broad Street, it looks like it was a wise move.
12-2am, club 7-2am, Sun 7 'til around midnight, bar noon-10.30.
£23.95 3-course meal

Someplace Else

**161-163 Broad Street
(0121) 632 6025**
The best drinking haunt on Broad Street,

www.itchybirmingham.co.uk

if only for the crowd that come here. Where else in the country do you find gurning ravers (pre-Bakers), moshing rockers (pre-XLs) and punters fondling themselves playing pocket snooker in gleeful anticipation (pre-Zig Zag strip club)? All three venues are within 20 yards of this bar, and this is the key meeting place, making it an earthy, no pretensions place welcome to all. Even better in summer when drinking spills out onto the Broad Street strip. And worthy of note are Beaujolais days in November – trust us.

Mon-Fri 9am-11.30, closed Sun
£5.95 Rib-eye steak with garlic butter. Also serve breakfast from 9am

Sports Café

Broad Street (0121) 633 4000

Sports Café, yes, but don't try turning up in your sports kit – this place is strictly Broad Street. No prizes for guessing the theme here, and they've really gone to town on it. Showing every kind of sport all the time – even in sport's darkest hours, they'll drag up re-runs of celebrity

crazy golf before the screens go blank. That aside though, this is one of the strip's more mystifyingly popular meat markets. Aside from the signed memorabilia of all descriptions (real F1 car, photos, cricket bats and what have you), there's a full-on dance floor should the bog-standard house and chart get you feeling funky. If it gets too much, recline in the leather chesterfields downstairs, light up a cigar and loudly proclaim "I could do better than that" when Ginola belts another shot wide from 30 yards. Does exactly what it says on the door.

Mon-Sat 12-2am, Sun 12-10.30. Fri/Sat £3 after 9pm, and over 21s only.
£5.95 Ball park dog (hot dog apparently)

Tiger Tiger

Broad Street, Five Ways (0121) 643 9722

Brum's very own bat-cave. You're met with a long, crowded bar with an older crowd (door policy is over 25s at the weekend) jostling for space as people walk back and forth. Everything is tall and airy; including some of the punters. This'd make it a fairly decent city bar if it stopped here. But float down the sweep-

ing stairs into an huge cavernous area set in maroon and tapestry, with grand alcoves at the side and tell me you're not impressed. Keep going – there's more. A stroll into what looks like the toilets leads you to a completely differerent laid-back brighter bar with chilled out funky tunes, Then, right at the back, in what looks like a fire exit, is a small passage into an industrial-style club. Suffice to say this place is so big, it comes as a surprise that you don't pop up in Selly Oak once you've walked the length and breadth of the venue. No draught at the bar means it can be quite pricey, but you can see where your money's going. Being a restaurant, club and bar all rolled into one means you don't need anywhere else. Mon-Sat 12pm-2am (£5 after 10), Sun 12-10..30

Pan fried fillet steak £12.95 (bar snacks also avail.)

▮ Walkabout

240 Broad Street (0121) 632 5712
'Aussie' hangout in the same way that Greg Rusedski is British. Like Australia, they're keen on big-screen sports and healthy-portioned food. However, unlike down under, they've got jet and ski simulators instead of the real thing, and they get shirty when you put your feet up on stools. Live music from time to time (often absolutely brilliant) and elbow-bashing jumping up-for-it crowds at the weekend. There's a club downstairs too; a fairly shonky affair we've written about in the clubs section. This place is best for its rugby internationals, and not for the Brummy staff trying to mask their accents by dropping "Sheila" into conversation.
Mon-Fri 12-2, Sat 11-2, Sun 12-10.30. £2 after 11pm and 9.30pm Fri/Sat
2-4-1 offers Sun-Thu

£4.50 Kangaroo Steak

▮ Wine REPublic

Centenary Square, Broad St
(0121) 644 6464
Attached to the Rep theatre is the Wine Republic (aka REP bar), but it would do a roaring trade even without the thesps. To fit in, it's important to bellow your order of dry white wine spritzers at the top of your voice, before bowing to the crowd behind you. Home to a large dining area and a glass-fronted bar, this place attracts those who know their Chardonnay from their Rioja, or at least those who think they do.
12-9.30 Rest, 'til 11am, some Sundays

£11.95 2 courses (Haddock fish cakes and chicken). HW: £9.95

14

52 Degrees North

**Unit 304, The Arcadian Centre, Hurst St
(0121) 622 5250**

Because Birmingham's 52 degrees north, obviously. And here marks the smoothest, most stylish, most slinky of all the bars in this city. If you can get past the door (Birmingham's only female bouncer possibly?), then you'll get to enjoy this lounge lizard's paradise with elegantly muted décor and dark cool corners in which to watch the pre-club crowd that drifts in and out. There's a long winding staircase upstairs and a ridiculously over-long entrance into this – well, they'd have it as a 1930's adaptation of a speak-easy, though it kind of reminds me of an upmarket low-lit airport departure lounge. Music is as relaxed as the chairs – low-slung acid jazz piping away in the background through those speakers that look like toilet seats. There's a suitably opulent bar, a fairly intimate restaurant and table service even for the drinkers.

Aside from the prices, everything is minimal, down to the tiny signs telling you which toilets belong to which sex. And yes I have, and yes they did shriek and no it wasn't funny. Sometimes, lounge bars can seem a little too sedate, but if that's what you're after, this has to be one of the best in the country. Best nights are model nights held once a month. Chances of getting in? 24 knock backs and counting...

Mon-Fri 5-1, Thu-Sat 5-2, Sun 5-10.30. £5 after 11pm

£17 for min. two courses, fillet of salmon with apricot and chutney (main)

TOP FIVE
Late-night bars

1. **52 Degrees North**
2. **Circo**
3. **Moneypenny's (w/e)**
4. **Someplace Else**
5. **RSVP**

Arca bar

The Arcadian Centre

Spankingly new addition to the laid-back lounge bars of the Arcadian centre. Looks like the Sobar, but even more stylish. It's still very early days for this bar, so it's currently devoid of people and atmosphere, but I reckon that's set to change. Full of subdued spot lighting, booth seating, and the odd curved slice

of wall throughout the place. Watch this space...

Bacchus

Burlington Arcade, New St
(0121) 616 7991

Exactly like the Medieval zone of the Crystal Maze, except Richard O'Brien won't be screaming that you've got 20 seconds left, nor do they do lock ins, more's the pity. Set underneath the Burlington hotel, high-backed chairs, suits of armour and tapestry on the walls help create this cosy and extremely popular city-centre haunt. Tables are small, meaning you find yourself joining in conversations whether you want to or not. The crowd is a melange of the young and old, united only by their high salaries.

Mon-Sat 11-11, Sun 11-8pm

£11.95 Breast of barbary duck

Bar Coast

The Arcadian Centre
Hurst Street (0121) 666 4931

One of the first bars in Birmingham, and they've refurbed to make sure they're

one step ahead of the game. Unlike a lot of haunts in the area, most people who go here remain for the night – settling into stylish surroundings and big tunes at the weekend. In the day, home to some decent 2-4-1 deals between 5 and 8pm weekdays, best experienced in summer when you can loll around outside on the tables. Floor to ceiling windows make it good for keeping an eye out for your mates.

11-11, Sun 10.30pm, 12 booze onwards 5-8 everyday 2-4-1.

£4 Samblas (Asian stir-fried dish)

Bar Med

159 Corporation Street
(0121) 200 1623

Blimey, I thought Bar Coast was colourful. So eye-poppingly rainbow-like, it's like taking an acid trip and flashing a torch in your eyes. The Mediterranean it most certainly isn't, but it could turn out to be a reasonable bar. It's still early days for this new addition to Brum's bar scene, and most seem to be sticking to the less gaudy, and infinitely more cool RSVP up

www.itchybirmingham.co.uk

the road. Still, there's a load of reasonable 2-4-1 offers in the day (5-7pm) and a decent line up of DJs from Thu-Sat, including James Bond from BRMB on Fridays. Check itchybirmingham.co.uk to see how it's faring.

Mon-Thu 10-11, Fri/Sat 10-12pm.
HH: 5-7 daily 2-4-1
£7.95 Chicken rimarno

Bennetts

Bennetts Hill (0121) 643 9293

Remember the Natwest advert with the old dear bemoaning that her bank has turned into a trendy wine bar? Well thank the Lord for internet banking because never has a trip to the Natwest been so much fun. A complete conversion, with giant ceilings and Georgian plaster work, together with huge Greek mythological murals on the wall, you can't fail to be impressed with the effect. Multi-sectioned, with tons of seating, snugs and a boardroom that ten of your friends can take over without having to hire in advance. As the surroundings suggest, attracts a young, affluent crowd.

Mon-Fri 11.30-11, Sat 12-11, Sun 12-5pm
£4.65 Chilli bowl with rice

Circo

6-8 Holloway Circus
(0121) 643 1400

Were it not for Circos, Birmingham would be back in the stone ages. Now just over five years old, this place was the first to tirelessly campaign for a 2am licence, finally opening the floodgates for the plethora of bars in the city. Despite its age, it's still one of the best. Dress code is like the place – smart and funky. It's one of the best places for kick-starting pre-club drinks, with music at the weekend ranging from house, blues, acid jazz – just about anything with rhythm. Sofas mix with a balcony upstairs, iron staircase and a crowd that reflects the time of day. This place is anything from a chilled-out coffee house in the afternoon to a full-on club-like atmosphere on the nights – the Technics mixing championships have been held here for the last few years and it's set to stay. Class.

12-2am, Sun 12-10.30pm. Fri/Sat 10.30 £2
Drinks promos 'till 11pm.
£5.50 Mussels with fries

The Cube Bar

Brindleyplace

A traffic accident of a bar. Could everyone stand clear while we try injecting some hardcore house? No joy? OK, liven

the crowd, get them jumping. "Whooh, whooh, wave yo' hands in the air!". Not working? Right, start bringing in a younger crowd – that's right, 18, 19, 20 year olds, that's good. Yes, yes, crowds of girls in bikinis in winter, but what's that? They're not staying. Right, try the promotions – £1 a drink nights has got to do it. No? What's wrong with these people! Call in the receivers, I think we've lost it.

Henry's

1 Victoria Square, Hill Street
(0121) 200 1136

If you're from the old-school of drinking, you'll be spitting on the floor of Henry's, what with their la-di-dah cocktail list, bloody water features, tossers in suits, expensive drinks prices, fancy staff who know their wines. But, for those who don't baulk at living it up at the weekend, you'll enjoy this refreshingly laid-back but vibrant bar.

Mon-Sat 6-11, Sun 6.30-10.30pm
£16.50 Set meal per head.

The Green Room

Hurst Street (0121) 605 4343

Friendly café bar catering to a mixed gay/straight crowd in the centre of Chinatown. Recently refurbished and now including a small dance floor, this place is an excellent chill-out venue with decent food to boot. It's pretty much all

seating, with table service, pitchers of beer and music that comes second to audible conversation. A true café bar, incidentally not green in the slightest.

Mon-Wed 12-11, Thu 12-1am, Fri/Sat 12-2am, Sun 12-10.30
£7.25 Hot spicy chicken breast

IceObar

16 Hurst Street
(0121) 622 6878

Right then, let's get this straight. McClucksy's is for the f**k or fight brigade, but IceObar isn't. Since the God-awful hell-hole round the corner opened up, a few stragglers found their way into this hefty and stylish mecca at the start of Hurst Street, but fingers crossed this isn't a trend – this place is one of Brum's better nightspots. Music nights vary from

TOP FIVE
Happy Hours
1. **Key Largo**
2. **Casa**
3. **Bar 260**
4. **Grosvenor Casino Bar**
5. **Bar Coast**

salsa (Tue and Sun, complete with lessons) to garage and although it's open 'til 1am, it's often used as somewhere to meet up for the clubs or casinos roundabouts. Usual Hurst Street prices, a stylish and monied crowd, and a select few who take advantage of the big open spaces to pose for England. Best on Saturday nights with Dave Clarke (Galaxy FM) educating the masses with eclectic house tunes.

11-11, apart from Sun 6-10.30

£4.75 Cajun chicken

Medicine Bar

**The Custard Factory, Gibb St
(0121) 693 6333**

Who'd have thought that a Bird's Eye custard factory would make way for a crowd of beatniks in what can only be described as the new Moseley? The bar is an odd mix of sofas and steel chairs set on two floors with a small dance room but it seems to work. Home to the modern millennium hippies in the funkiest, alternative dance, acid jazz kind of way. Instead of lime Bacardi Breezers think absinthe, with a sprinkling of feng shui and tantric sex.

Mon-Fri 11-2, Sat 7-2, Sun 6-10.30

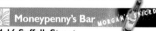

Moneypenny's Bar

**14-16 Suffolk Street
(0121) 633 7770**

Like a VIP cocktail lounge, only they seem to be running out of VIPs during the week because it's often empty. It's no bigger than an independent clothes shop, and although it's done out in a suitable cool and laid-back fashion, unless the place is packed, it lacks soul. When it's a bit empty, it gives you that faintly sick feeling before a party when you're not sure if anyone's going to turn up at all. Get there at the weekend though and it's a different story, with Fridays seeing Human Nature – a night with some of the best club tracks around. It's a venue bar – ie, people don't stumble into it, so the crowd are a friendly laid-back bunch. Incidentally, the rumours about this place closing are outright lies – it's actually getting bigger and better all the time, so shove that in your pipe and smoke it.

Mon, Tue 5-11, Wed-Sat 5-2. No food

Quo Vadis

190 Corporation Street (0121) 236 4009

Drawing in the law crowd from the surrounding courts during the day and a more fashionable set (or maybe they've just gone home and got changed) during the evening. Spacious wooden décor with long trestle tables does sound a bit Firkin-like, but this place is far better than

popular, hot and stuffy. Bottles are recommended if you want to keep your 1664 away from your threads.

Mon-Wed 10-11pm, Thu-Sat 'til 1am

£4.25 Soup noodles

Sobar

The Arcadian Centre
(0121) 693 5084

A bit like an underground car park, except the spot lighting's more flattering than neon strips and the entrance doesn't stink of piss. It's essentially a noodle bar, but at night the food is swept away in favour of a chilled-out pre-club or post-work crowd. Bears an uncanny resemblance to the Arca bar across the way, but Sobar were here first. Have a fairly non-commercial mix of laid-back tunes in the day and DJ'd funk, soul and big beat come the weekend. Best moments are in the summer, when the terraced seating allows you to watch the variety of free laid-on entertainment in the square. Except when Barrymore shows his face.

Mon-Sat 12-2am, Sun 12-10.30

£5.95 Hofan beef and spinach

that. DJs or bands on Friday and Saturday nights keep the place lively, and maybe because it's a bit out of the way, attracts a more discerning and friendlier crowd than Broad Street.

Mon-Fri 11-11, Sat 6-1pm closed Sun

£6 Burger and chips

RSVP

186 Corporation Street
(0121) 236 1945

The bars in Birmingham are getting better and better – and this is one of the best. A large open-plan light and airy feel make for relaxing afternoon sharpeners, and the sunken area with leather bean-bags are top for drunken slouching. It's got all of the décor and atmosphere of a Broad Street bar at a fraction of the

price. Food is typically of the pasta-perfection ilk (or pasta-ponce, depending on your tastes). The nights make way for a pre-club crowd where it gets immensely

Slug & Lettuce

17 Thorpe Street
(0121) 622 5659

One of the All Bar One-esque bars in town, with the tried and tested formula of lots of shiny surfaces pine wood and wrought iron chairs. Now chain places like this can be bland as you like, but the S&L have got it just about right – at least in Birmingham. Tapestry malarky adorn the walls, and a young attractive crowd fill the place throughout the week and cram

www.itchybirmingham.co.uk

in at the weekends. Friendly and efficient staff, mostly catering for a pre-club crowd. Good for a more sedate afternoon with the papers during the day.
Mon-Sat 12-11, Sun closed

£5.95 Sausage and mash (12-3 only, not Sat)

The Temple

Lower Temple Street
OK, now call your parents and tell them you're in trouble. This is a temple for only the most hardened worshippers, and you should dwell on the fact that the path of the righteous man is beset on all sides by the antiquities of the selfish and the tyranny of evil men. And they all live here.

 Yates's Wine Lodge

190 Corporation Street
(0121) 233 9378
Whoops, you've walked into the wrong place. Retrace your steps and cross over to the Crown – this is a chain bar so far past its sell-by date that it's been festering away at the back of the drinking cupboard like that nasty Ouzo you brought back from Corfu. Yates's of course has absolutely nothing in common with a wine lodge. DJs at the weekend, hot from the latest weddings, serve a mix of bland chart tunes to suits and hen parties. Bacardi Breezers sold by the tart load, naturally, except during the suited and booted lunch hours during the week.
Mon-Sat 11-11.30, Sun 4-10.30
Sun-Thu Happy Hour all day Fri/Sat 2-9pm
£3.95 Wholetail scampi

Outside town centre

It's saying something that there's only one bar in the whole of Selly Oak, Moseley and Harborne. This should be a clear message to wannabe bar owners – gap in the market anyone? We know that the council equate alcohol licences with selling their soul to the devil, but there's only so many times they can say no...

The Cross

Alcester Road (0121) 449 4445

Looks a bit like a kitchen, what with the large ventilation shafts and pine tables. It had to happen eventually, and this is Moseley's first place to eschew grunge for clean lines and a fresh bar feel. Admittedly, it doesn't have much competition, but it's still an excellent bar that would be just at home in the town centre as Moseley. The chrome bar serves all kinds of beers, including those funny unpronounceable Belgian ones. Downside? At the weekend, the whole of Moseley reckons they can fit inside and squash up the place like Broad Street.
Mon-Sat 10.30-11, Sun 10.30-10.30
Jerk chicken with wild sauce £8.50

pubs

www.itchycity.co.uk

City: Aston Triangle

Right by the university, and little else, this place is heaving with students and children in need of a pint.

The Black Horse

Jennens Road, Aston Triangle
(0121) 359 7108

An "It's a scream!" venue. Really? The fact that this pub is within stumbling distance of one of Birmingham's busiest roads so that students can play in the traffic? Or that the 'beer garden' is more of a tiny Aussie outhouse? Attracting the none-too-fussy students of Aston and UCE, this place is aimed at squeezing every last penny out of grant cheques. Gaudy bright colours, masses of promotions (with their Yellow Cards, available for a quid if you show your NUS card), a handful of pool tables (one L-shaped) and a small venue upstairs for the odd live band or special one-offs. The punk scene moved on a long time ago from here, leaving the usual smattering of students. But ignoring its fume-choked location, it's a lively and raucous affair that does well for itself, because there are no closer alternatives.

Gosta Green

Holt Street, Aston Triangle
(0121) 359 0044

Yet another Firkin converted to an "It's a Scream!" theme pub, but this place is an improvement on the style of old. Like the whole area surrounding Aston, the buildings look like the urban sprawl of Full Metal Jacket. So it's quite surprising that the Gosta is half-decent. Typically, they've painted as much of it yellow as they can get away with, but thankfully, you won't have to put up with the wacky students guffawing over giant Jenga anymore. It's friendly and welcoming, with more than enough room in this huge L-shaped pub to accommodate the masses of students. They've a beer garden too – actually, more of a skanky patio with outdoor heaters.

Sacks of Potatoes
10 Gosta Green, Aston Triangle
(0121) 503 5811

In summer, this place can do no wrong, slapped outside the Aston Union and with plenty of space on the grass triangle outside for everyone to roll around in the sun, and er...dogshit. Inside it's a much more local affair, where Brummies take refuge from the hordes of hokey-cokey dancing medics recounting their latest urinary tract operation. Not much in the way of theme nights, or space for that matter, but that's its beauty. Old-style juke box keeps the older students and locals happy.

City: Broad Street
Bright lights in the big city, with just about every chart tune available. Wear smart shoes, because as you full-well know, trainers are a sure-fire way of marking out would-be gun-toting underground mafia. Nowhere likes big groups of lads either – separate into twos and threes.

All Bar One
The Waters Edge, Brindleyplace
(0121) 643 8633

All Bar One's are not known for their sparkling originality, but this one hits the spot. Gets as busy as is physically possible with queues after 8.30, maybe because it's about the only place you can still have a conversation as they don't crank the tunes up to Merchant Stores' level. Looks exactly as you'd imagine with lots of tables, fast and efficient service and absolutely no surprises whatsoever.

Brasshouse
Broad Street (0121) 633 3383

"Do you like my tits?" she gurgled as I walked in, and then promptly rejoined the other ladeez to shimmy the lambada with that guy from accounts she'd always had her eye on. Full of a bolshy crowd who remember the 60s the first time

around, and so towny that townies are afraid to drink here, unless fully equipped with statutory white shirt and chinos. Chart music at the weekend (what else?) together with enough Brylcream to stick your feet to the floor. You're better off using the main doors to reach the fantastic Celebrity Balti house above.

The Comfort Inn

Station Street (0121) 643 1134
For those desolate souls catching the last train out of Brum, a chance to reflect and drown your sorrows before you board the 12.07. For those just arrived, you should really get out more – it's under a bloody train station for crying out loud. Otherwise known as Platform 13.

Fiddle & Bone

1 Sheepcote Street (0121) 200 2223
Set up by two string-pluckers from the CBSO orchestra, this pub aims to bring their music to a wider audience – kind of, because although you won't find the entire orchestra ensemble playing, you do get regular live music every night from folk to jazz. Couldn't be more different from the rest of Broad Street and is brilliant in its own way. Older and more beard-stroking crowd than its young surrounding upstarts, but still lively as you like. You'll be old one day too, remember.

Figure of Eight

236-239 Broad Street (0121) 683 0917
The McDonalds of the brewery world have opened up in Broad Street too with their mind-numbing formula of no music but cheap pints. The old-school (I'm sure they boast 'traditional' décor of patterned carpets and bog standard tables) does nothing to lift your spirits, but the prices probably will. Open at 7am for breakfast (but not alcohol, clearly).

James Brindley

Bridge Street (0121) 643 1230
When Central TV produced more programmes from Birmingham, this place used to be home to all the stars, from Bob Carolgees to Bob Warman – you couldn't move for Z-list celebrities. Times have changed, but the pub hasn't really. Quieter than the rest of Broad Street, and a bit older too, this place has an ever-changing crowd, surrounded by glass and steep pint prices. Overlooks the canal in places, so you can have a bird's eye view of those shopping trolleys winging their way past you. Nothing special.

 **Galaxy 102·2 THE NEW MIX FOR BIRMINGHAM**

The Malt House

Brindleyplace (0121) 633 4171

Off the beaten track, but no worse for it. Great views over the canal, with a crowd slightly older than the rest of the cocktail-glugging shiny orange clintele of Broad Street. As they'll never tire of telling you, this is where President Clinton had his fish'n'chips and a pint when he was here for the Birmingham Summit. Allegedly, his cronies also had to smash the plate and glass afterwards to ensure that traces of his saliva couldn't be used to incriminate him in another Lewinsky-type scandal. Distinctly plausible by the side of the canal of course, where plenty of cigars are smoked.

The Old Monk

230 Broad Street
(0121) 633 380

Cockney rhyming slang as far as I'm concerned. This place doesn't really fit into Broad Street, not sure whether to draw the curtains and light candles or throw the doors open and large it up for the weekend. So it doesn't do either, and attracts a crowd of punters umming and ahhing where to go next. No food. One of these days, I'm going to spray an 'ey' at the end of their name.

O'Neill's

Broad Street (0121) 616 7821
Mon-Sat 11-2am

They've recently refurbed and revamped O'Neill's, and done a smashing job, with a much-improved bar downstairs and another upstairs. Somehow they've managed to wangle a 2am license for what is

still essentially a pub. What's more, it's free everyday, except Fridays and Saturdays when it's £5 after 10.30pm. During the week the music's 60s, 70s and 80s, bringing it a bit more up to speed at the weekend with more modern stuff. Still, nothing too taxing, and although it's less of the craic than the other O'Neill's near the Arcadian, with pub, pints and cheesy music, you can't go far wrong.

Pitcher & Piano

Brindleyplace (0121) 643 0214

This place has seen a number of name changes, but this is one of its better reincarnations. Two floors and you can drink just about wherever you please – the downstairs is no longer for dining only. Pitcher & Piano is another big corporate chain, based on the pine and chrome formula tried and tested by ABO opposite. But, to make them stand from the crowd, they've got a piano the crazy cats that

they are. Not sure why they bother, because it's not like you get discounts for playing it, even with my jazzed-up version of chopsticks. They might want to spend the money on some more draught lagers – 1664 only. Inoffensive.

Tap & Spile

Gas Street (0121) 632 5602
All the flashing neon of Broad Street can feel like a poor man's Vegas after a while, which is half the reason the Tap does so well. Far-removed from the banging beats and cocktail pitchers around the corner, the Tap is a genuine old-style canal-side pub with nooks, crannies and a whole host of 'stars' from Central TV who make this their local. This is the kind of quaint tavern that all Americans think is typical of England's pubs. If only...

Name, ages and occupations?
Sarah (left), 22 Book-keeper, Dawn, 28, Hotel receptionist
Favourite shop? H&Ms and Top Shop
And where do you rock? XLs
No surprises. And drink? Walkabout
Best nosh? Athens restaurant
What do you love about this city? It's always lively, and oh, those baltis...
And what don't you? There's no decent alternative pubs

Central

Bier Keller (Mr Bill's)

Suffolk Place (0121) 643 5830
If you're getting married, you've just turned 18 or you're into table-dancing (no, as in dancing on tables), the Bier Keller serves up nights of frothy steins and German frump. Tatty from the outside, but typical piss-up party on the in.

The Crown

Hill Street (0121) 616 7801
There's nothing fancy here, but then that's why it's quite handy. If you've had a sordid night, are sick of the bright lights and thumping beats of Broad Street and need to sort your head out before trying to appear normal at work on Monday, come sit down, open the paper and unwind, as old fellas around you chuff on their pipes and tell you how the world used to be a better place when UB40 were touring. Now, feeling better?

Factotum & Firkin

23 Bennetts Hill
One of these days, they'll run out of "F"-words and will have to name one the Fanny & Firkin. Mind you, although the

number of Firkin pubs nationwide is enough to sap your will to live, this one is well worth the effort. The old bank conversion may have a fairly small capacity but the place is immense – with a roof as high as a church hall and a cosy second level that allows you to flick peanuts onto punters below. The only downside is that on ground it feels a bit soulless unless it's packed out – usually only on nights with live gigs. They're trying to attract a business crowd, but they might want to note their shamefully shit T-shirts proclaiming "I'm a Firkin Multi-Talented Bar Steward" are unlikely to be a hit. Massive projector screen sports and usual pub grub.

week with the finely tailored crowd excitedly talking shop, but dies down to a slow murmur at the weekend as the less successful come to recount their disasters of the previous week.

Newt & Cucumber

58 Stephenson Place
(0121) 643 2969
Where else can 'boast' bouncers from 12 midday? It's shocking that they need them, but they're a good bunch – unusual for a town centre. To be fair, it's a pretty good oval affair, firmly aimed at lads being dragged on shopping trips with their better half. A Blackpool-esque array of gamblers, video games and big screens, set in the large open spaces, with snugs and alcoves for smaller groups or couples. Gold trimmings and pub carpets abound, with karaoke on a Thursday, 80s Friday and 70s and 90s on Saturday. Good for football and food, with a happy hour 2-7 weekdays.

Hill Street Q's

78 Hill Street (0121) 643 0431
Pool halls never attract the most salubrious of crowds, and Hill Street is no exception. But what it does, it does quite well – a whole host of pool tables, a crowd ready to hustle and snacks like pizzas and burgers from a measly £3. Don't worry about making an effort – no-one else has.

Hogshead

29 Newhall Street
(0121) 200 2423
Suits, chairs and a relaxed and monied crowd. It's near the stock exchange area, so you can forgive the talk of buy, buy, sell, sell... maybe. Wine-cultured and sophisticated, it's heaving during the

O'Neill's

19 The Arcadian
(0121) 666 4951
An Oirish pub begorrah! But before you write it off as yet another plastic paddy pub, give this one a chance, as it's the

most authentic of all the O'Neill's. Formerly Pat O'Connells, they've changed the name but lost none of the vibe. Live Irish and folk music all year round attracting a lively and up-for-it 20-40-year old crowd. Watch out for Two Pats – two Irish fellas as good at comedy as music. Fantastic.

Old Joint Stock

4 Temple Row West (0121) 200 1892
Set in the 'lovely area' of Pigeon Park, this is another converted bank with loomingly high ceilings, sizeable square bar and a traditional pub-style atmosphere. Owned by Fullers, brings a taste of London into Birmingham, so drink the lager instead. Nothing too out the ordinary here – the daytime crowd of suits and Rackhams shoppers are quickly replaced by a pre-clubbing crowd praising the talents of Craig David. Hmm...

PJ's Moon & Sixpence

The Arcadian, Hurst Street
(0121) 666 4941
A tasty boozer, and true enough you have to be tasty to drink here too. The place has history, but don't ask about it – it's best left forgotten.

Sam Wellers

Hill Street (0121) 616 1731
I've no idea who Sam Weller really is, but I'd imagine he's a hoary old scrote that hangs around Digbeth Coach Station. It's opposite a multi-story car park for starters, and it smells of wet dog. Full of the sad, desperate and dejected, and even though there's cheap beer, DJs at the weekend and karaoke on Thursdays, you should still remain firm. Pool tables and a lack of a will to live complete the effect.

The Shakespeare

Lower Temple Street (0121) 616 7841
Sometimes you might be in town waiting to meet someone, and you fancy lapping up a touch of culture while you wait. Well, if you're after a spot of thew Midland's favourite playwright, a visit to the Shakespeare might suffice – there are pictures all over the wall of literary memorabilia. Of course, it does help if you're not only bored and old, but also hard as nails. Attracting more the Iagos than the Desdomonias of this world. Best in summer, when you can sup in the sun.

www.itchybirmingham.co.uk

Sputniks

Temple Street (0121) 643 0426

Most likely last refurbed when Sputnik were in the charts, this is the authentic underground indie bar of Birmingham. Wannabe pop stars who worship NME and embrace unemployment cram into this tiny underground pub cum bar every night, packing it out at the weekend. There are always DJs, with open deck slots on a regular basis for you to impress the crowd with your crossmix fade of Black Sabbath and Britney. There's a door policy of 'no daft drunk lads'. Or fat people come to think of it – the toilets are tiny.

Square Peg

**115 Corporation Street
(0121) 236 6530**

"The longest bar in Birmingham" they shout. And it's got to be one of the cheapest. As it's a Wetherspoons pub, you can get a burger and pint for £3 – now ah kid, any blowke with no spondooliks has gotta luv that. In fact, several do – usually old ones, chuffing away on a pipe and dribbling into their pint. Done out in your old-fashioned carpets and wood and handy as a meeting point, this place is busy, without fail. Despite its size, it's always hard to get a seat, except in the ominously quiet no-smoking section. No fuss, no frills and of course, no music. Often full of Villa fans after the match.

Toad

16 Hurst Street (0121) 633 9584

They've taken the "slurping" out of the Toad, and following its extensive refur-

bishment, now is more in keeping with the rest of Hurst Street. There's a huge screen on the second floor banging out sports all through the day and night, but it's not exclusively a hero-worshipping venue. Depending on the night, acts as a pre-club venue for Zanzibar, DNA's or even McClusky's. Recommended.

The Trocadero

Temple Street (0121) 616 2631

Completely unlike other city centre pubs, the Troc is home to a friendly atmosphere for the 20-35 crowd. There are two distinct sections – a dressy pine-floored clean bar-like area as you walk in, and an enormous carpeted snug at the back complete with big screens and grungy students. If the Ralph Laurens and stilettos of town get too much, here's somewhere cool for respite. Used to be really grungy, but is now a touch smarter.

The White Lion

**The Horsefair, Bristol Street
(0121) 629 1071**

Back in the old days, crowds of up-for-it revellers would meet here, looking gormlessly at one another without speaking, as the speakers thundered out

the latest chart classics, warming up the crowd for the tack-fest of the Dome II. Now the Dome has shut (too much violence apparently), this pub is a complete waste of space. DJs at the weekend try to create a club atmosphere in what is still a pub, no matter how many flashing lights and MTV screens they stick in it. The only relief is in summer, when the patio garden is open for some top drawer sun-drenched drinking.

Yard of Ale

New Street (0121) 616 7901

When the glaring lights of New Street shopping become too much, seek out the Yard, tucked away down the stairs away from the crowds. Suffered in the hands of the '74 pub bombing, but it still remains an institution on New Street. It's two flights underground and fairly typical for a city pub, but it's cracking. You'd miss the door if you weren't looking out for it, but look closer – it's well worth it. Blues pub, with big screen sports from time to time. Clientele range from your pissed grandad telling war stories to kids hoping to get served more than a McDonalds. Football colours best avoided after 4.45pm. Seriously.

City: St Paul's

The Rope Walk

St Pauls Square (0121) 233 2129

Like a lot of places round St Pauls, busy in the week, quieter come the weekend. Banks pub with no surprises – well, except there was the 'Hokey Cokey' sounding out of the function room last time we went and an old fella throwing a cowboy hat around, but that's not a weekly occurrence.

Jamhouse

1 St Paul's Square
(0121) 200 3030
Mon-Sat 12pm-2am

Strictly speaking more a club and restaurant than a pub, but it opens at 12, which is early enough in our books to consider it a good drinking den. See the club section for more info, but suffice to say this is one of the best places to relax around St Paul's – always friendly, always happy and particularly on the night, a smashing atmosphere. Aside from the full-on restaurant, bar snacks are available throughout the day.

Mongolian, St Paul's Square, Xanadus

Ludgate Hill (0121) 236 3842

These three all sit together like peas from the same pod, with the three doors sitting side by side. Xanadus is a fairly innocuous affair serving pricey deli-type food. The real draw here is the two bars St Paul's and the Mongolian. SP's is a pre-club bar, choc-full of MTVs and a hardcore raving crowd, while the Mongolian is the usual Mongolian affair (that's get

www.itchybirmingham.co.uk

TOP FIVE
City centre pubs
1. O'Neills (Arcadian)
2. Newt & Cucumber
3. Factotum and Firkin
4. Toad
5. Yard of Ale

your own food, and see if they can be bothered to cook it, for the uninitiated), Tasty – with as much as you can eat for £5.95. Can't be bad.

Harborne
Home to the Harborne pub run, which is now officially illegal – so don't try starting at the far end of Harborne working your way down to the White Swan/Dirty Duck will you?

The Bell
11 Old Church Road (0121) 427 0934
I'm sure this place has been lifted from Heartbeat. Next to the old church and bowling green, this is so homely, you wander why it's opened as a pub. The bar is a bar in the loosest sense of the word that fits no more than three people, and as with all such tiny places it's very much locals. Keep the noise down kids.

Fallow & Firkin
359 High Street
(0121) 426 1048
Bad, bad, bad. For starters, it was better as the Kings Head before Firkin got their grubby mitts on it. But even so, it's crappy position and many, many more credible alternatives mean that come the fall of the Firkin empire, this one should be one of the first to be culled.

The Green Man
2 High Street (0121) 427 2690
They've had their seemingly annual refurbishment (they never seem to leave it alone), and they've knocked through the two bars into one large one, stamping themselves firmly as the busiest pub in Harborne. Young and old mingle happily together, and for a more sedate afternoon there are plenty of snugs and corners for quiet chat with roaring fires in the winter, and a central fighting area for the lairy. One of the best pubs in Harborne, with a massive car park to boot to finish matters with blades and shooters. Being Harbourne, more likely to be cross words and angry stares, but still.

The Harborne Stores

109 High Street (0121) 427 0971

Small and inoffensive, full of the elderly and infirm bemoaning everything from the rising price of petrol to horror stories of West Midlands transport. Also home to that ever entertaining game, "What's under my hat today?".

The Junction

212 High Street (0121) 427 0991

Decked out just like a Firkin, only a hell of a lot better. One of the best in Harborne that's home to a whole host of decent bands. Last visit saw a bunch of 'crazy' dance students forming a human pyramid, only for one to fall and break his wrist. So it's also home to good karma.

The Old House at Home

193 Lordswood Road (0121) 427 8756

This Toby Inn hasn't changed in years – the clean-cut entrance bar for the older

crowd, and the lounge area for the younger ones. It's cosy, it's comfy, it's unobtrusive. You feel like you could put your feet up and have a little kip.

The Varsity

186-192 High Street (0121) 4264256

Décor is "industrial on a shoe-string" ie tries hard but it's a bit crap. The youngest crowd in Harborne, and you'd stick a fair chance at pulling were it not for the thundering handbag house and cheese anthems drowning out your efforts. The largely student crowd are of the type that don't need loans, grants or any other funding, so don't believe their impoverished stories of hardship – they're most likely to be blagging a free pint. Good honest fun.

The Vine

310 High Street (0121) 426 0901

This big one-roomed pub is quite a smart effort in Harborne, and like many of its neighbours, attracts that Harborne-type crowd – ie early 30s with a large sprinkling of couples. There's a small conservatory out the back (la-di-dah eh?) and all in all, it's a harmless, inoffensive pub.

The White Horse

2 York Street (0121) 427 6023

Real ales old fella's haunt with one bar

plit across two rooms. Full of the locals happy to chat and have a game of cards. Now settle down and have a pint or two, but not too many – might interfere with the dominoes. Steady...

The White Swan/Dirty Duck

Harborne Road (0121) 454 2359

The only pub with two names, depending on whether you're coming from town or Harborne. The jolly hockey sticks and excellent rugga old-boy's network mix in with an equally affluent local Harborne crowd. They're doing their utmost to attract families at the moment, with a separate dining and carvery area, but the place still has its charm as a real pub. Almost entirely seating areas, carpeted, low wooden beams – you get the idea.

Moseley

Bulls Head

St Marys Row (0121) 449 0586

Oldest pub in Moseley and one of the oldest in Brum. As we all know old doesn't necessarily mean good though. Rough round the edges, stinking toilets, local crowd 35 plus. Never likely to win any awards, but then I don't suppose they care. A local pub for local people. You're not from round these parts are you?

Fieldmouse & Firkin

St Marys Row (0121) 449 0811

In the old days when it was The Fighting Cocks, you used to get a spliff and fight

free with every pint. Sadly, those days are long gone, and the mammoth Firkin chain waded in and sanitised the whole lot. Still, they haven't totally destroyed the atmosphere – still very much a grungy/indy-type hangout with live music, Old Harborne and men with dogs on bits of string. Big screen sports from time to time and cinema evenings sponsored by the local Cinephilia video shop.

Hogshead

Salisbury Buildings, Alcester Road (0121) 449 3340

It's a chain pub but don't let that put you off. Young indies and beard-strokers mix happily together in this bright and friendly boozer. Always sociably busy and serving up cracking-value food. The only downside is that it's not so good that it's worth enduring the standing-room only weekend crowds.

Jug of Ale

43 Alcester Road (0121) 449 1082

For those Wednesdays when only a £1 in, £1 a pint and a free DJ and live band

Find places for late drinks on your WAP
wap.itchybirmingham.co.uk

will do. The Jug of Ale in its various guises has more town-centre feel than the other places in Moseley, except when there's live music. Upstairs has seen the likes of Oasis, Ocean Colour Scene and uh Clemency – a mix of the up and coming and down and out. Other than that, it's a multi-platformed pub with great big glass windows and a typical grungy Moseley lot. Now there's so many more places in town, a steadier local crowd have moved in and are settling in nicely.

Prince of Wales
118 Alcester Road (0121) 449 4198

The heart of the Moseley community. It's old, it was the first place in Birmingham to get Guinness on draught (and now the best), and it's still battered round the edges. There's an old geezer's front bar, cosy lounges at the back the size of a small living room, and a big beer garden / patio (best for the summer eh?). Don't expect expensive refurbishments, but credit to the friendly management, staff and punters, this place always does well for itself.

Old Moseley Arms
53 Tindell Street, Balsall Heath
(0121) 4401954

OK, so not quite Moseley but not far off. Worth including because it's such a

beautifully-kept traditional pub. As it's a bit off the beaten track, the friendly crowd (nudging late 20s and early 30s) are usually here for the night, so the atmosphere is relaxed but vibrant. Large beer garden with sports and pool room, live music, open mic and ... just get down there. Absolutely top.

O'Neill's
93 Alcester Road
(0121) 442 3901

Signs helpfully pointing the number of miles to Kilkenny – much as I'm sure there are signs in Kilkenny pointing to Birmingham. Ignoring the faux-Irish theme, this place is the busiest in Moseley – probably due to the location. Crowds vary and it's a hit and miss affair – when it's Moseley people it's a cracking place, but when gangs from Druid's Heath decide to descend it gets far too lairy/did you spill my pint/come and have a go etc. Heated beer garden, stage for some dubious bands in the past and floor service – great idea, but you spend half your time chasing the buggers round trying to catch them to take your order.

Patric Kavanagher
Woodbridge Road (0121) 449 2598

Veterans of Moseley will remember the place as the drug-infested loony-hole

gies and dregs have gone, and this place is waiting for a new crowd to make it their home. Great food and karaoke night on Thursday; the only place I've ever seen a bespectacled middle-class white kid bitch into the mike "I'm the Slim Shady, the real Slim shady mo'fo!".

▉ Selly Oak

▢ The Bristol Pear

676 Bristol Road (0121) 414 9981

Sister pub to the Gun Barrels down the road, it's more of the same but in a smaller and more laid-back fashion. Similar student-friendly prices (with Yellow Card discounts), same garish décor and less likelihood of pissed-up rugby players mooning at you over a pint. Couple of pool tables and usual big screen sports.

right next to the police station (beggars belief I know), formerly known as The Traf. However, a fair amount of refurbishment has turned this into one of the best pubs in Moseley. The beatnik feel is still preserved with live music and functions upstairs in the S2 room (home to the world's smallest dancefloor for everything from drum'n'bass to latin nights), and the atmosphere is all good, all days, all the time. There's an L-shaped bar for the majority, and a smaller yellow-flavoured conservatory at the back if the music's not your thing. Only downside is that it gets elbow-jammingly pint-spilling-ly busy at the weekend.

▢ The Village

Alcester Road (0121) 442 4002

My word, what's happened here? The Village used to be the life and soul of Moseley, but poor management, some unfortunate crowds and increased competition has meant the biggest pub in the area has died a slow and mournful death. Huge car park, massive lounge (still good for big game sports – you can see the screen from anywhere) and a tatty bar. Even on a Friday it only takes one barman to serve everyone, it's that whisper-ingly quiet. On the upside, the kids, drug-

▢ The Brook

Bristol Road (0121) 414 9911

I remember the days when you'd walk in and bottles would whistle past your ears as the locals playfully bounced students off the walls. But there were bad times too, and it's about time this place got seen to. Far less troublesome that it used to be, but permanently smelling of sick – how do they do that? It's empty most of the time, which is madness considering the weekend usually sees queues outside the Gun Barrels. Apparently, it's going to be converted into a sports-themed pub shortly – the sooner the better. Currently, by unspoken agreement, the front bar belongs to the locals.

Goose @ the OVT

561 Bristol Road
(0121) 472 3186

Once the highest grossing pub in Europe, the Old Varsity Tavern was Firkinised (or Firk'd up depending on who you talk to) a couple of years back. Its newest incarnation is as one of the Goose range of Wetherspoons pubs, offering the various charms of just such an indentikit establishment: cheap beers (£1.30 a pint) and spirits, quick and inexpensive menu and no jukebox. The wooden floors have been replaced with carpets and it's a cosier affair than the previously overbearing Firkin. If you want a quiet pint, join the couple of old boys drinking a pint of cheap mild in the corner.

The Gun Barrels

Bristol Road (0121) 471 2672
As with all 'It's a Scream' pubs, they paint as much of it banana yellow as they can

get away with. Despite the residents protests, they've made this once dingy and murky boozer into a bright and incredibly popular student haunt that brings a bit of life (read 'vomiting and sex in pub car parks') to a quiet area. Heavingly busy every day except Monday and Tuesday, this is the mecca for most students – especially the 1st Years. It's a big place with large seating areas, yellow lighting in tin barrels swinging from the ceiling, pool tables, games and the obligatory Yellow Card discounts for NUS holders. Big screen sports, naturally, and if the music's pants, blame the bar staff.

TCs

Coronation Road (0121) 472 0939
Although this place is membership only, the crowd is probably the best in Selly Oak. The membership business is to get around the residents protests (remember this next time you're spangled shouting in the middle of the road). It's free to join (you can sign two people in on your card) and well worth the hassle – the mostly 20s and early 30s crowd is happy and lively, especially when there are functions in the back room. Watch out for drink promos, sports days, pool tables and table football. Home sweet home.

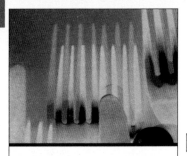

restaurants

www.itchycity.co.uk

We've chosen the best restaurants in town, together with a sprinkling of those in our selected areas of Harborne, Selly Oak, Moseley, as well as the Balti Triangle in Sparkbrook. As a quick guide, if the phone number starts with a 6, it's centre of town, 2 it's towards St Paul's, and anything else, you might need to check your A-Z.

American

T.G.I. Fridays
180 Hagley Road, Edgbaston
(0121) 454 1930

TGI's – at its best it's a place to go and let your hair down put on stupid hats and have a big party meal with alcohol in equal proportions to your food. At worst, it's like one of those cringy American sitcoms when they can't stop hi-fiving each other. "You are SO the money baby". That said, staff are friendly, some with permanent fixed gurning grins like they dropped a few Es before they started their shift. Ten out of ten for effort and around six for the food.

Meal for two: £24.29 (American hot chicken sandwich)

McClusky's Bar & Restaurant
Smallbrook Queensway
(0121) 616 3939

Restaurant my arse – serves food, that in my opinion like the clientele in this hell-hole, is manky, skanky and best left untouched.
Meal for two: For two? Tell me you're joking.

Chinese

Down by Hurst Street and in the surrounding area is Birmingham's Chinese quarter, Chinatown. Not quite as plentiful as London's, but nevertheless packed with plenty of Eastern delights.

Chung Ying Garden Restaurant
17 Thorpe Street (0121) 666 6622

The undisputed king of Chinese restaurants, this massive two-floored palace of a place is a must for fans of oriental food: it's well worth ordering your basic Chinese dishes just to see how much better they can be cooked by the experts. Full of Chinese diners which is always a reassuring sign. Try their fantastic seven-course set meal for two

although I defy you to finish it (Moseley's Rugby Club prop forward couldn't manage it, so take that as a challenge). The crispy duck and plum sauce is among the best things I've ever tasted whilst the service is crisp, efficient and unobtrusive.

It's easy to sound gushing about a place like this; it has all the ingredients for a cracking night out. Quality of food is second to none but remember that the prices do reflect this.
Meal for two: £32.50 (Chichen chow mein)

China Court Restaurant
24 Ladywell Walk (0121) 666 7031

You're not going to miss this place in a hurry, housed in what looks like a Chinese palace right next to the Arcadian. It's authentically-styled (I've got no frame of reference here, so I'll trust them on that), and inside the place is absolutely mammoth. The menu is confusingly large, with over 100 dishes to pore and comb through, before you eventually settle for a set menu for fear of ordering something unpalatable. You needn't worry mind, as the food here is exquisite and full of flavour. Chinese food when done properly should taste like this, and if you're prepared to be abysmally disappointed with every takeaway you taste after this, then you should sharpen your chopsticks and come rushing in. Not cheap by any means, but food of this quality rarely is.
Meal for two: £22.50 (Sweet and sour chicken)

Henrys Cantonese Restaurant

27 St Paul's Square (0121) 200 1136

As you approach the grand green pagoda entrance, you'd be forgiven for thinking that this place houses an infinitely stylish eatery, but you'd be wrong. It's disappoint-

ing inside (smacks of a chain restaurant, which it is) and in the winter, finger-freez-ingly cold. Although I can't exactly knit jumpers with noodles, I reckon I'm up there with the best of them. However, the chill was making it hard to speak, never mind eat and I couldn't get a grip on my sticks. They brought a fan heater to be fair, but it's not quite what you want. Inside is a little cramped – better for Inuit couples than parties and the food was at best, OK.
Meal for two: £15.80 (Canton special fried rice)

Tin Tins Canteneese

The Waters Edge, Brindleyplace
(0121) 633 0888

None of your flock wallpaper and fans in here – this cavernous one-room affair is a modern take on Cantonese-style food. Romantic it most certainly isn't, with lights so bright they could double as heaters. So assuming that doesn't put you off, you should come here for the food and food only – it's excellent value and delicious, particularly the lunch menu. All the portions are generous and well-cooked, and it might not serve to impress your partner, but it will impress your taste buds.
Meal for two: £29 (Sweet & sour pork)

Wing Wah

Chinese Restaurant Unit 1a, 278
Thimble Mill Lane, Nechells
(0121) 327 7879

Aside from the great name, this is a place where food takes precedence over serv-ice, surroundings and even the cus-tomers. Attached to the Wing Yip super-market, you can bet your Ying and Yang that the produce is fresh and sure enough, our visit laid out some of the most exquisite Chinese food I'd ever clamped my teeth on. However, it's mod-ern looks and brisk service feels a bit soulless and rude at times, and the place is a bit of a trek on the outskirts of town. We were about the only two non-Chinese customers, which may go some way to explain why we were treated like freaks of nature.
Meal for two: £24.60 ($1/4$ crispy duck)

www.itchybirmingham.co.uk

All Bar One

Brindleyplace (0121) 644 5861

This popular bar and restaurant chain has an acceptable menu with friendly, efficient service and serves food until ten. The menu comprises a few carefully chosen contemporary classics, the Thai noodles with king prawns being a particular favourite. Drinks come direct from the bar where the selection of wines is extensive: the house Chardonnay is an inexpensive choice at £10, while the £15 Chablis is also worth a punt when you're feeling a bit flash.

Meal for two: Ham and eggs (£25)

Bennetts

8 Bennetts Hill (0121) 643 9293

See the bars section for more, but this place is a perfect respite from the New Street hustle and bustle to indulge in some fine cuisine. Unlike many of the bars on Broad Street, food here isn't a frozen ready-made meal whacked in the microwave and passed of as a fresh home-made dish. Oh no, they actually

take some time and attention over their food, and it shows. Gordon Bennet indeed.

Meal for two: £28 (Pork menu)

Bucklemaker Wine Bar & Restaurant

30 Mary Ann Street, St Paul's Square (0121) 200 2515

In the well-heeled St Paul's area, you expect restaurants to be both expensive and luxurious – this one succeeds at the latter but is reassuringly good value too. Best seat in the house is in the refreshing wine cellar alcove – though you can eat at the bar, and there's a more formal dining area at the rear. Food is healthily portioned (none of your slim slivers of salmon here). We went for the tapas dishes, providing us with more than enough to shunt around the

remains at the end of the meal. Attracts a lot of suits as you might expect, but also couples and families. Obviously the word is out.

Meal for two: £39 (Fillet steaks)

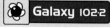

Café Face

519 Bristol Road

Another good spot for a quick lunch in Selly Oak, again based on the Bristol Road. It's nothing special, but remains an institution in the area – students latch on to these places like lifeboats. There's an average range of sandwiches, baguettes and baked potatoes alongside the biggest latte I've ever tried to drink. Prices match the student clientele and you'd be hard pushed to spend more than a fiver before exploding. Hasn't made too much of an effort on décor with plastic chairs and table cloths, but I guess you get what you pay for.

Mere shrapnel for greasy breakfasts

Leftbank Restaurant

79 Broad Street (0121) 643 4464

Because it used to be a bank you see? Ho ho. Ignoring the miserable play on words, this is a jewel in Broad Street's already

pretty jewel-laden crown. Classically swanky to the point where trainers and jogging bottoms will be met with gasps of camp horror. So for maximum entertainment, you should dress up in your shellsuit and demand the finest seats in the house.

Once they know you're serious about eating here, they'll treat you with a modicum of respect. But ignore them, because the food's awesome – braised pigs' cheeks with foie gras anyone? An eclectic off-the-wall menu with prices and attitude that reflect its wadded clientele.

Meal for two: Around £30 (currently serving 2-course set menus for £24.50, House wine £11.50)

Mud Café

570 Bristol Road, Selly Oak
(0121) 472 7790

The Selly Sausage's posh neighbour, this lunching establishment is increasingly popular with both students and local businessmen for its great range of coffee and excellent, inexpensive (£5 or less) pasta and panninis. Penne with chicken, ginger and spinach is a particular favourite, while for veggies, the gorgonzola and brocolli pasta should not be missed. A friendly and uncomplicated place, the seating's all on long wooden tables which you'll regularly share with other diners.

Meal for two: £10 (chicken as above, excluding wine)

The Selly Sausage

539 Bristol Road, Selly Oak
(0121) 471 4464

A true student institution, set up by an ex Brum Uni couple years ago. The murals of Bob Marley and Jim Morrison give it a grungy student feel, whilst the wide variety of fry-ups, burgers and baguettes make it an ideal place for the morning after the night before. The American pancakes are a big enough draw in themselves, but it's worth going just to see the fantastic cook, who is a dead ringer for Uncle Monty from 'Withnail & I'. The Selly Oak experience would not be complete without a visit.

Burgers and baps, cheap as you like

St Paul's
St Paul's Square (0121) 605 1001

Situated, as the name suggests, in St Paul's Square at the heart of the newly developed Jewellery Quarter, this small and elegantly furnished bar and restaurant

provides a moderately priced and excellently prepared variety of contemporary cuisine; whether you're after wonderful pork and leek sausage in port gravy with garlic mash or an excellent chargrilled salmon steak, the quality is consistently excellent and the service slick and friendly. The wines are well chosen and can be ordered directly from the bar, lowering the cost of the meal considerably whilst in no way compromising the quality.

Meal for two: £27 (Stuffed chicken breast)

Wine REPublic
Birmingham Repertory Theatre, Centenary Square, Broad Street (0121) 644 6464

See bar section for more. Food varies from salmon to chicken though there's not too much space inside – booking's advisable.

Meal for two: £28 (Salmon)

Seafood

Oceanic Restaurant
90-91 Livery Street, off St Pauls (0121) 236 7500

There are no other seafood restaurants in Birmingham, so in theory, Oceanic could get away with anything. But it's hard not to describe the place without gushing – so fashionably beautiful, with glass ceilings and a breath of modern air, everything has been carefully designed to look and feel perfect, from the huge wine

And you are? Al, 19, Student

I say. Favourite place for a brandy?
Gun Barrels on the w/e before Frenzy

And for a banquet? Chamon Balti house in Selly Oak

Your favourite shop? Virgin

And for the foxtrot? DNA on a Tuesday

Best thing about Brum? Well, friendly and caters for students

And the worst? Either the accent or the weather. **What d'yow meen kidda?**

glasses to the stunning lights that reach right down to your table and service that's difficult to fault. Still small enough to remain intimate, large enough to show off their striking metallic décor, and moreover you'll experience the most mouth-wateringly tasty seafood in Birmingham. OK, not the greatest boast as there's no direct comparison, but suffice to say this place is highly recommended, and no I'm not being paid. Honest.

Meal for two: Around £30 (Currently serving 3-course meals for £20, House wine £11.25)

Needless Alley Fish Restaurant
10 Needless Alley (0121) 643 4775

Fish and chips used to be the staple diet of every Briton. Sadly, the days of fish and chips wrapped in a copy of the Sun are long gone, but for a more hygienic but just as tasty meal of the basics cooked with flavour, crack on to Needless Alley (off New Street) for a taste of our country's finest dish. Takeaway or sit-down – one for lunchtime rather than a romantic tete-a-tete, unless she enjoys pies, sausages and grease, and if she does you probably won't want to be seen in public with her anyway.

Mexican

Poco Loco
40 St Mary's Row, Moseley
(0121) 449 3259

Walk across the road from Bistro Lyonnaise and you'll find its antithesis. A triumph of image over substance, Poco Loco seems to subscribe to the "sit 'em down, serve 'em fast, get 'em out" philosophy, and before you've had a chance to say "That was crap!" they'll slap the bill on your table. The usual variety of fajitas, tacos and chilli dishes are served at slightly inflated prices and it's not entirely satisfying. On my last visit the heat of the food came almost exclusively from the spices, the temperature of my tacos being at best tepid. For that extra minutes walk go French instead. A shoddy, shonky effort that's not worth bothering with.

Meal for two: £35 (King prawns)

Bank Restaurant & Bar

4 Brindleyplace (0121) 633 4466

Because a place has an ultra-modern décor, 'exclusive' prices and a good reputation, you'd have thought it would be one of the finest in Birmingham. Food-wise, it was delicious, but you feel you're

paying a lot for the stainless steel wall and 'fashionable minimalism' But the real problem is the service – polite and well-staffed yes – but so unbelievably hurried it beggars belief. A full 3-courses in under one hour isn't on, and at these prices you expect to be able to come for a night out. The tables are really close together (intimate, yeah?) and with such a high turnover of customers every hour, you feel that money comes before the cus-

tomers. Kind of like a bank in fact.
Meal for two: £35 (Chargrilled chicken)

Berlioz Restaurant

**The Burlington Hotel, 6 Burlington Arcade, 126 New Street
(0121) 633 1737**

Overlooking the delightful New Street which, although admittedly better now it's pedestrianised, is still not the ideal backdrop to the 'understated elegance' of the Berlioz with the post-pub mooning crowd. Not only is the Burlington the city's most luxurious hotel but the Berlioz is one of, if not the poshest restaurants. Food was melting with flavours and the service was impeccable – especially when a spot of oaf-like behaviour saw a full glass of Rioja fall into my loved one's lap, and the waiter honourably tried to take the blame for it. She didn't buy it, but thanks for trying fella.
Meal for two: £43 (Duck)

Bistro Lyonnaise

**13 St Mary's Row, Moseley
(0121) 449 9618**

Set right at the heart of Moseley village, you'd not be the first to assume from looking at the exterior of this small French bistro that it was thrown together in an afternoon. However, what the exterior lacks, the interior more than makes up for: an intimate and friendly little outfit owned by local foodies which serves up unpretentious, well-cooked rural French cuisine. Whether you go for the excellent variety of set menus or choose from the à la carte, you'll not go hungry with portions that are a far cry from nouvelle cuisine. Bags of character, and weekend booking essential.

Meal for two: Around £30 (Currently serving 3-course meals for £19.80, with House wine served in 1-litre carafes for £12)

Café Rouge

The Waters Edge, Brindleyplace, Broad Street (0121) 643 6556

Low-lit lights, romantic atmosphere and shonky food – my last visit went to confirm my profound suspicion of the chain as a whole. If the triumph of French food is ordinarily the elegant and thoughtful production of good uncomplicated grub, for my money this place fails on every count. The blackened salmon with lime and noodles appeared to be a barely recognisable incinerated piece of fish accompanied by undercooked noodles lathered in Rose's cordial. The pleasant efficiency of the service hardly compensated for a highly under-whelming dining experience. Which makes it mind-boggling that you have to book as it gets exceedingly busy.

Meal for two: £29.50 (Lamb gigot)

Chez Jules

5a Ethel St (0121) 633 4664

Tucked away off New Street is Chez Jules, and after a makeover at the start of the year (they got rid of the graffiti – shame), they've added a raised seating area for more intimate dining. The main dining area is a bit too open and canteen-like, but that's about the only criticism of the place, with classic French food served up in a suitably swift and jovial way. The maitre-de seemed overly bossy, reminding me of the guy in those French textbooks that was always smoking a pipe when the wife was washing up and doing his cooking, but the other staff didn't seem to mind. Excellent food with a wide variety of flavours and textures – one to seek out.

Meal for two: Around £30 (Currently serving 3-course meal with fillet of red sea breem for £17.50. House wine £7.95)

Le Petit Blanc

9 Brindleyplace (0121) 633 7333

For a place as gastronomically inhibited as Birmingham once was, the arrival of one of Raymond Blanc's small band of high quality bistros came as an unheralded surprise. Despite the man's name and

reputation, Le Petit Blanc, tucked away in Brindleyplace just off Broad Street, is a far from intimidating environment in which to enjoy fairly-priced and fantastically cooked rural French cuisine. Don't bother to dress up in this unpretentious and

elegantly understated restaurant, simply enjoy the quality of both food and service. In comfortable harmony, old classics like coq au vin sit next to rarer delicacies such as the fantastic bouillabaisse I had on my last visit. At around £15 for a main course the place is also surprisingly inexpensive and the sommelier has constructed a fantastic, if somewhat more extravagantly priced wine list.

Meal for two: £39 (Rib eye steak)

Michelle's La Bastille Restaurant Francais

220 Corporation Street (0121) 236 1171
69 High Street, Harborne
(0121) 426 4133

Both have the same kind of menu but different atmospheres – the one in Harborne is tiny, best suited to quiet and intimate dates, while the Corporation Street branch is more boisterous and

lively. These are rustic, rickety wooden-floored places with your red checked tablecloths and authentic French cuisine. Food here is smashing, with an excellent à la carte menu, carefully and thoughtfully presented. I was especially impressed by the best moules marinière I've had in this country. The wine list is, however, best consulted only after a call to the bank manager, presenting a not wildly interesting array of the usual old favourites at rather steep prices. Overall, nothing too fancy about the atmosphere, but plentiful and tasty food. Recommended.

Meal for two: £26.50 (Beef bourgignon)

Indian

As many a Brummy knows, this city is where the balti dish all started. As such, there are hundreds of restaurants everywhere, and it's as much a part of Birmingham culture as the Blues or Villa. The best restaurants are in Sparkbrook – not the most salubrious of areas, but when you're half-cut or after good food, who cares? They form the so-called 'Balti Triangle', formed by the Stratford and Ladypool Roads and Stoney Lane.

Adil's Balti

148-150 Stoney Lane (0121) 449 0335

These people have a lot to answer for. Back in 1976, they opened up the first ever balti-house in the UK, bringing their special style of cooking to Brum (originating from Baltistan, Kashmir) and now look at the place! Balti refers to the fact that the food arrives in the balti dish (so therefore fresher), but also to the cooking from this region. Anyway, suffice to say, a finer curry in Birmingham is hard to find, and the same family is behind the fantastic selection of dishes available. It's scruffy, no frills BYO (there's an offie across the road). Not extravagantly decorated or priced, but comes so highly recommended you'd be churlish to ignore it.

Meal for two: £11 plus wine (Chicken tikka jalfresi)

Chamon
507 Bristol Road, Selly Oak
(0121) 472 1698
Selly Oak's finest balti palace, but don't expect a table come 2am as the place is regularly packed to the gills with students wishing to get some ballast after a night at the union – legend has it that many a union night ended with Gary Glitter's 'Come On' drowned out by the raven-

ous roar of "Chamon Cham-on", a reputation richly deserved. This is not to say that the place is best frequented when drunk as both the traditionally ornate

curry house décor and the friendly staff contribute as much to the experience as the compendious and excellent menu. If you really can measure a curry house by its Chicken Tikka Masala then I can do no better than to recommend it here whilst their infamous family naan should not be attempted by parties of any less than eight unless you also want to camp out under it.

Meal for two: £14 plus wine (Chicken tikka massala)

Diwan Restaurant & Takeway
3 Alcester Road, Moseley
(0121) 442 4920
A bit further out from the main strip of Moseley is the Diwan, but it's worth that extra walk for the real balti dishes. We've had literally countless meals here, and they've always been up to scratch, with the difference between the dishes being more than a sackful of curry powder. With over 100 seats you can always get a seat, and it's probably Moseley's finest.

Meal for two: £8 plus wine (Chicken korma)

Celebrity Balti
44 Broad Street (0121) 643 8969
Post-pub baltis are ten a penny, but good ones in the centre of town are hard to come by. Bizarrely, the place is decked out like an English Lord's dining room, replete with pictures of royalty adorning the walls. The food however is authentically the best balti you can get outside of Sparkbrook. Despite the location, the crowd doesn't tend to descend into the usual post-pub 11pm dribbling wrecks

you might expect; they're probably put off by the regal feel. The food's well worth seeking out – bit on the pricey side, but it's got to be worth the extra few quid to get a really tasty meal.

Meal for two: £21 (Vegetable balti)

I am the King of Balti's
230-232 Ladypool Road, Sparkbrook
(0121) 449 1170

I'll be the judge of that. Aside from the name, this is a typical Sparkbrook balti house, with typically Indian-styled interior set on the murky Ladypool Road. It's a BYO, but they'll chill your wine if you ask them nicely. Food here, like most of the houses in the triangle is top drawer, but I wouldn't say they're about to win any Michelin stars and King they are not. Maybe third to the throne. Particularly intriguing are some of the more unusual dishes off the thorough menu – 'balti meat with lady's fingers' anyone?

Meal for two: £11 plus wine (Balti meat rogan josh)

J Jay's Indian Restaurant
2 Edgbaston Shopping Centre
(0121) 455 6871

Oh the glory, the fame. The proprietor here has met John Major and is seen here shaking hands with the fella, all over the walls. Much as I'm sure Major has pictures of the proprietor all over his gaff. But that aside, the marble exterior and tall chairs and plush surroundings set a rather more sedate restaurant feel (as opposed to the post-pub lagerthons of others). Next to Regards, and lots better, both in terms of settings and food.

Meal for two: £23 (Chicken curry)

Jewel In The Crown
125 Alcester Road Moseley
(0121) 449 4335

Licensed restaurant slap bang in the middle of the Moseley pub run, so it does a roaring trade most nights. The owner here is the most mild-mannered and friendly fella in Moseley – we've seen him deal with abuse of the worst kind on Friday and Saturday nights and he takes it all in his stride and nothing seems to dampen his spirits. You can see through to the kitchen to check on the progress of your balti (but no, they don't want to check on the progress of your piles while you moon at them – what is it with rugby lads?), and the food here is always respectable – if a little forgettable.

Meal for two: £17.50 (Chicken korai)

Khanum

**510 Bristol Road, Selly Oak
(0121) 471 4877**

Chamon's poor cousin, this is really a balti greasy spoon, complete with plastic table cloths and chairs. That said, the service is speedy and the baltis not bad at all as long as a little grease doesn't bother you.

As with many of the Bristol Road balti houses, four people ordering main courses will ordinarily receive complimentary popadoms (or if you're pretty or lucky or pretty lucky, onion bhajis). Hygiene is good and the one time I was exceedingly ill here probably had a great deal more to do with the umpteen pints of lager I'd had than the meat madras.

Meal for two: £9 plus wine (Chicken korma)

Maharaja Restaurant

23/25 Hurst Street (0121) 622 2641/3113
This place has won a whole host of awards, (real ones from Ronay, Michelin and Good Curry Guide as opposed to their good friend, the chef). It shows too, for this is a well-established restaurant, with fine, fine food that is all too often experienced lashed up when it should be

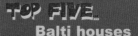

sampled sober. Good value prices, cheesily grinning waiters and a vibrant atmosphere. We like.

Meal for two: £24 (King prawn curry)

Milan Indian Cuisine

93 Newhall Street (0121) 236 0671
If the thought of yet another normal Indian does nothing for you on the night, then the Milan might be the answer. Offering dishes with a twist on the normal run-of-the-mill balti cuisine using exotic herbs and spices adding a special flavour to your favourites. Despite the fancy gourmet action, the prices aren't much fancier. Worth it.

Meal for two: £21 (Garlic lamb)

Regards II

**9-10 Hagley Road, Edgbaston Shopping Centre (nr Swallow Hotel)
(0121) 454 0061**
Now the Broad Street branch has closed, they've opened up a Regards II. Like Karate Kid II, you wonder why there was ever a sequel as the first one was a bit shit anyhow, but like the Godfather II,

www.itchybirmingham.co.uk

this one is better than the first. Nothing to really separate it from the multitude of other curry houses, and with its location, you'd have thought it'd be packed out every night, were it not for the superior J Jay's a stone's throw away.

Meal for two: £24 (Chicken massala)

Royal Naweed Tandoori

44 Woodbridge Road (0121) 449 2156
Royal Naweed say that they will cook your meals exactly as you want them. They also say they will cut your throat if you don't pay the bill. Like the Jewel in terms of the abuse they've received over many drunken weekends, but more like Samourai Warriors in their response to trouble. In terms of food, there's little to distinguish between this and the Jewel just down the road.

Meal for two: £8.50 (Chicken jalfresi)

Shimla Pinks

214 Broad Street (0121) 633 0366

"Let me see that thong" crooned Sisqo as we were seated at our table. A curry house of firsts if ever there was one –

despite the delapidated exterior, inside is the plushest curry house in Birmingham , seeing the rich, wealthy and famous dining on extravagant and delicious food. No pretensions (they played his entire album) but with image-conscious and dressy décor and clientele. Service is just

the right side of obsequious and the food itself does justice to Birmingham's reputation as the Balti capital of the land. I find it hard to resist the tandoori mixed grill, whilst for non-carnivores, the mushroom, spinach and potato balti is a must as long as you are in no rush to walk away from the table. Singing along with tunes incidentally, is not the 'done thing' as we found out to our chagrin. "Oooh that dress is scandalous"...

Meal for two: £36 (Tikaty Jinghey, a jumbo king prawn-based dish)

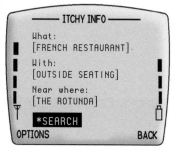

```
 ———— ITCHY INFO ————
 What:
 [FRENCH RESTAURANT].

 With:
 [OUTSIDE SEATING]

 Near where:
 [THE ROTUNDA]

 *SEARCH
 OPTIONS              BACK
```

**what you want
when you want it
eat out using your phone
wap.itchybirmingham.co.uk**

Spice Avenue

562-564 Moseley Road (0121) 442 4936
Sounds like some horrendous set from Spice World, but this place is a far cry from the has-been slappers of yesteryear. Silver service isn't something you expect from curry houses, as any visit to the Balti Triangle will testify, but obviously they saw a gap in the market for the well-to-do to feel well-heeled in a well-nice restaurant. Somewhere to go for a fully-fledged night out, where the meal is the focus of the evening rather than an inebriated post-pub afterthought. Prices are surprisingly reasonable too, considering the quality.
Meal for two: £21 (Balti chicken with seasoning)

Directory Restaurant and Bar

**103 Edmund Street, Colmore Row
(0121) 236 2620**
A dull-sounding title for a wonderful restaurant. A favourite among the office workers in the surrounding area, this is a fairly priced, elegantly modern restaurant (don't let the outside fool you), with flavoursome wordly-sounding dishes (Grilled red mullet fillets anyone?) that met all of our expectations. There's a mind-bendingly long wine list with around two hundred wines in stock, and I must admit they did roll their eyes a little when I asked for the house white. Service was suitably discreet yet attentive, and the tiger prawn cakes will definitely make me return. And I'll order the house white again, sod you all.
Meal for two: Grilled fillets (£35)

The Jam House

1 St Paul's Square (0121) 200 3030

 **Galaxy 102·2 THE NEW MIX FOR BIRMINGHAM**

Jools Holland's plush bar and restaurant comes complete with an evening of live entertainment from the wide variety of soul, funk and R'n'B bands that appear nightly. A booking at the restaurant guarantees an enjoyable way of gaining free entry and missing the ever-present queues. Inside, the cool décor and pleasantly spacious seating area adds to a well-constructed contemporary menu encompassing a wide variety of American and World cuisines. To be honest, you come here because you love the live music – it's a full-on night out – but that said, the fairly limited menu offers some standard dishes but done exceptionally well. It's possible to eat in the bar area, but we recommend booking and getting a table, as bar seating round the side is a bit squashed. One word of warning – the service can be a bit too laid-back and un-attentive. Mind you I'm used to being ignored.

Meal for two: Around £40 (currently £35 for 3 courses)

Metro Bar & Grill
73 Cornwall Street (0121) 200 1911

Hmm, Michelin liked it. The press love it. And it's always busy, so it feels a bit tight to start knocking the place. Inside, it's a beautifully designed place, with an oval opening in the roof and stunning artwork adorning the walls. But that doesn't make it an ideal restaurant – they've placed the bar and grill right next to each other, so the noise of one drowns out the other. It's fine if you're in a large group but if you're a couple you find yourself shouting to rise above the cacophony round

the corner. Food is expensive for what it is, and I know that surroundings count for a good part of this, but you feel that it's a bit over-inflated and from my experience over-hyped. It flatters to deceive – the Stan Collymore of Birmingham restaurants.

Meal for two: £31 (Smoked chicken)

Tai Pan
1st Floor, 2a Wrottersley Street
(0121) 622 3883

The same guy who owns the fantastic Suko Thai in Solihull now owns this place

and it shows, with a tasty variety of Chinese, Thai and Korean food all served up in this groovy restaurant. Needless to say, the variety of dishes will have you umming and ahhing for ages, but we've never heard a bad word said against this place. Prices here verge on the tremendous for the quality of food, and for eastern delights, there really is little competition.

Meal for two: £26 (Stir fry chicken)

Italian

Bella Pasta

102 New Street (0121) 643 1548

For that "don't know where to go and am bloody starving moment", located half-way up New Street. The service here really is surprisingly good and attentive for a chain restaurant and while the menu is hardly likely to throw up any major surprises, what it lacks in originality it makes up for in convenience. Good range of pasta and pizzas (big fan of their spicy tomato and pepperoni pasta), but the beer is surprisingly expensive.

Meal for two: £22 (Spaghetti bolognaise)

Caffè Uno

126 Colmore Row (0121) 212 0599

A nationwide chain of cheerful Italian-themed cafe/restaurants. An impressive and expansive menu, well-priced with generous portions. There's the expected range of pizzas, pastas, gnocchis and bruschettas, but also a range of fish dishes too. It may not be gourmet, but it certainly won't be too harsh on your wallet either. Great for those ad-hoc meals when you need to get out without making too much of an effort.

Meal for two: £23, Calzone al formaggio

La Galleria Restaurant & Wine Bar

Paradise Place, Paradise Circus
(0121) 236 1006

Pleasant, if unmemorable, restaurant within spitting distance of Paradise Forum opposite Gio's. It's surprisingly big and surprisingly bland inside, but the food was reasonable in a kind of shrug your shoulders "I've had worse" kind of way. And so were the prices.

Meal for two: £38 (Steak)

Little Italy

2 St Mary's Row, Moseley
(0121) 449 8818

The name is entirely accurate as the place is both small and comfortable and

CAFFÉ UNO

The Only Italian You Need To Know

126 Colmore Row, Birmingham B3 3AP

Tel: 0121 212 0599

www.caffeuno.co.uk

run by a friendly bunch of Italians who live locally, serving real Italian produce. You don't pay over the odds for the privilege either: starters at £3.50 to £6, main courses starting at around £8. There's an excellent range of pasta, including daily specials (the seafood linguine being particularly good) whilst the pizzas are fantastic. Two things are particularly great about this place – firstly, the owner who comes round and talks to the customers is just about the only one who ever does in Birmingham, and deserves credit for it, and secondly, the old cellar downstairs which is infinitely better than the ground floor, complete with fountains and a taste of true Italian atmosphere. Top drawer. BYO too.

Meal for two: £22 (Chicken cashatora)

San Carlo Ristorante Pizzeria
4 Temple Street (0121) 633 0251

Located just off New Street, this is one of the most central restaurants in town and is now no longer a well-kept secret, serving to large-scale corporate parties as well as romantic meals on account of the high seating capacity. There's Italian directors, Italian management and Italian chefs – so OK, it's quite Italian in here. The place is very Roman, with marble pillars and a baffling array of mirrors, but it's got a good atmosphere. The menu is predominantly French and Italian with a good variety of fairly standard main courses and starters, most notable for their excellent preparation and the generosity of portions. The desserts are particularly worth a mention, being both fantastic in quality and variety: the

tiramisu must be tried to be believed. You'll find prices on the extravagant side, but you're paying as much for the exuberance and style as you are for the food.

Meal for two: £31 (Pasta with lobster)

Valentino's
73 Harborne High Street
(0121) 427 2560

Next door to Michelle La Bastille, this friendly and well-patronised Italian serves the usual array of Italian dishes, although since refurbishment it does seem to have a few gastronomic delusions of grandeur, especially with its terrace – a collection of garden-centre conifers which occupy part of the High Street and serve as scant partition from the High Street itself. That said the service is efficient without being too intrusive. The food was excellent on the occasion I visited, especially the excellent salmon and wild mushroom tagliatele. Especially popular at lunchtime where a large proportion of the nearby Queen Elizabeth Hospital's medics can be seen (and heard) lunching and if the vivid description of colostomy operations doesn't put you off your food, enjoy!

Meal for two: £26 (Tagliatele)

Japanese

Shogun Teppan-Yaki
The Waters Edge, Brindleyplace
(0121) 643 1856

Not to be confused with the Teppan Yaki house in the Arcadian centre, the Shogun joins a number of other high-class restaurants by the canal. Suitably plush as you might expect, here you get to see your food cooked at your table. This isn't because they're lacking in kitchen space – it's part of a style of cooking derived from the name of a warrior. Who presumably cooked at the table, yeah? The largely wealthy and sophisticated diners pack this place out most of the week, so book well in advance. Lightening-fast service, pleasant and courteous, and mostly un-warrior like.

Meal for two: £34 (Shredded beef-based dish)

Teppan Yaki
Arcadian Centre, Hurst Street
(0121) 622 5183

Lots of partitioned walls in black and white, and packed out with distinctly wealthy couples. Maybe it was a special monied dating agency night as you don't have to be dripping in gold cards to eat here. Food arrives sizzling and fresh – just as it should be, but the atmosphere was on the wrong side of quiet, even for an intimate meal. Tell you what, get some big bass speakers and start pumping out Ricky Martin – oh, no, that's Las Iguanas across the road.

Meal for two: £25 (King prawns)

Mediterranean

52 Degrees North
The Arcadian Centre, Hurst Street
(0121) 622 5250

See bar section. Style-wise, you'll either slide in and feel right at home or you'll perch awkwardly on the side-lines, depending on your tastes. Food ranges from the refreshingly inventive to the seemingly overpriced, largely depending on whether you like the place. Our Thai fishcakes were perfect, but hey, you're entitled to your own opinion. Upshot of all of this is get to the bar, have a drink, and if the whole swish scene turns you on, stay for a meal. Otherwise, there's always Mr Egg outside.

Meal for two: £35 (Fillet of salmon)

you've tried this one...now try them all 17 other cities to indulge in

Casa Paco
7 Fletchers Walk (0121) 233 1533

Reassuringly Spanish in both décor and ambience, this place is a fine institution in Birmingham's restaurant scene, with its white stucco walls and arched windows. It's pretty small, with intimate little tables and a veering towards tack on the walls but no matter – the food here is second to none. A comprehensive menu serving up everything from monkfish to chorizo sausages all of which are rather exquisite. Prices are very reasonable, service extremely friendly and to be honest, the night would have been perfect were it not for the gangly guitarist who arrived on skateboard and 'serenaded' all and sundry with his wonky renditions of Spanish classics. Even Gloria Estefan would have been better, but still – the place is recommended nonetheless.

Meal for two: £30 (Paella)

Ipanema
60 Broad Street (0121) 643 5577

The girl from Ipanema lived the high life in Brazil, lapping up the sunshine and easy-going vibes, so you'd expect much the same from this spanking new edition to Broad Street. It's both a restaurant and bar with a small dancefloor and DJ whose Latin flavours keep them grooving all night (well, at the weekend anyway). Dividing into two halves; the front lounge, bar, dance floor and raised restaurant, plus a more intimate hidden restaurant round the back. The food here is tremendous, and amidst a multitude of posh restaurants, it is both unique and worthy of a visit for all occasions.

Meal for two: £27 (Jerk chicken sandwich)

Las Iguanas
The Arcadian Centre (0121) 622 4466

In the centre of the Arcadian development, this Latin American restaurant provides a cool terracotta and primary-coloured backdrop to a wide array of Mexican and Andean fare, dominated by a plethora of meat dishes for the enthusiastic carnivore. Service is ordinarily quick and efficient although on one occasion I waited half an hour for a luke warm steak which the staff were not at all happy to take back. "You eat it then." Vegetarians may find Las Iguanos somewhat limited with those dishes available rather smelling of a grudging and unimaginative concession.

Meal for two: £22 (Enchiladas)

Old Orleans
80 Broad Street (0121) 633 0144
See bar review for this authentically tacky experience of the deep south. But if all their food tastes likes this, Jamie Oliver could make a killing giving them a few lessons in basic cookery. Do not burn food! Serve it hot! Make it tasty! All pretty basic culinary skills you'd have thought, but sadly they haven't got to grips with any of them. And complaining doesn't help much either – she looked at me like I just threw her wage packet into the canal.

Meal for two: £27 (Mushroom chicken with mushroom, funnily enough)

Quod
Broad Street (0121) 643 6744
Oxford's excellent Mediterranean eatery has come to Birmingham, and we should be welcoming it with open arms. They've gone for the modern art, bright and airy feel rather than recreating 'authentic Italian' in keeping with the rest of Broad Street, but this is definitely a plus. Kind of feels Mediterranean, at least until you see it tipping down through the huge windows overlooking the strip. The food, as with the Oxford branch, is nothing short of excellent – with the exception of some pricey bottled beers, prices are excellent value for a whole range of dishes, most of which you wouldn't find in your standard eatery. I can particularly recommend Risotto with roast pumpkin and garlic, just as I can recommend spending a night out here.

Meal for two: £25 (Spanish torpoleni)

Pizza

Pizza Hut
98 New Street (0121) 643 1241
Unit 202 The Arcadian Centre
(0121) 236 0221
Pizza Hut is Pizza Hut wherever you go, and although it's easy to slag it off lets face it, this place was home to many a first date when you were little nippers, so

give it a chance. Though those still separating the bill by saying "you had TWO cokes didn't you?" should be given a wide berth. Still, looking at it, it's surprisingly expensive for a non-too exotic pizza, especially when you can go to Pizza Express for more or less the same price.

Meal for two: £25 (American)

Pizza Express

Brindleyplace (0121) 643 2500

For those that don't already know, Pizza Express is a chain that does things with a lot more care and attention than the rest. As buildings go, this isn't necessarily one of the best (custom-built as opposed to a renovated old church or what have you), but it still maintains the same high standards and reasonable prices as the rest. Our only grudge, as with all PE's is that the pizza's look distinctly on the small side. Must be some n a t i o n w i d e shortage of bread I'd imagine. One of the more welcome chains along Broad Street and Brindleyplace.

Meal for two: £26 (American)

Bits 'n' Pizza

Broad Street (0121) 643 2648

"Why have we come here Jeremy?", nagged the haughty woman next to us. "It's not exactly relaxing is it, I mean really?". We felt like clocking her one to be honest – true, she had a point. It's not a place for romantic tête-a-têtes, but that doesn't mean to say it's not a fine pizzeria.

Set across two levels, this is a bright and airy place, probably best suited to big groups and those up for a laugh. Staff are impeccably efficient and friendly, and despite the name sounding like a shonky takeaway, the food was nothing short of delicious.

Jeremy, next time that old munter gets on one, file for divorce. One of the best value eateries on Broad Street.

Meal for two: £23 (Calzone)

www.itchybirmingham.co.uk

THE INDEPENDENT

THE INDEPENDENT
ON SUNDAY

why not subscribe and

save over 60%

For a limited period only, The Independent would like to offer you the chance to purchase The Independent & Independent on Sunday for only £1.50 a week, with our advanced purchase payment subscription. Payments can be made by simply telephoning

0800 783 1920

quoting REFERENCE ISO1000ITCHY

Offices open Mon to Fri 9am - 9pm, Sat & Sun 10am - 4pm

Answer machine at all other times.

clubs

www.itchycity.co.uk

Birmingham Academy

Dale End (opp. Toys'R'Us)
(0121) 262 3000

Older residents of Brum will remember that this place used to be home to the skanky, puke-infested carpet-shagging den of iniquity in what was then the Hummingbird. It closed down amidst tales of underage drinking, drug wars and dodgy deals. The Academy can promise no such salacious gossip, but it does see the return of a much-needed large capacity (2300) indie club. It's fairly simple inside – a huge stage, massive dance-floor, U-shaped balcony with minimal seating, a portakabin for a DJ box and a little side room playing more alternative alternative, if you catch my drift. As a club, it attracts a crowd of grungers at Ramshackle on Fridays and Blast on Saturdays. But where it really comes into its own is for live music – absolutely the best venue in Birmingham. With their links to Brixton Academy and the Empire in London, expect the coming months to draw in some of the finest acts about. Check itchybirmingham.co.uk for more details.

Tongue

Bakers

163 Broad Street (0121) 633 3839

Banging house and garage club that's one of the finest for the beepy crowd. Inside it's not that big – there's a small circular dancefloor, a couple of podiums for those who want to show their knickers to the world and a luxurious chill-out area. What little there is they do well. For this year, they've already lined up Carl Cox, Judge Jules and Dave Pearce to name but a few, and doubtlessly they'll continue to attract the hordes of dressy Evian-drinking, arm-waving gurners that pack this place out every weekend. Put on your finest glad rags too as the bouncers have been known to wander up and down the queues singling out the scruffy and unkempt – kind of like an adult version of the playground abuse of "you stink, live in a trailer and your mum shops at Aldi". Wednesdays can be a bit lifeless, but Friday and Saturdays more than make up for it. Pre-club drinks at Someplace Else.

And you are? Mark, 21, student
Where do you go for a tipple? Circo
Warming you up for? Sundissential
And then for recovery? McDonalds – rude not to. Sobar when I'm feeling plush
Where do you get your threads? Kensington Freak, everytime
Best thing about Brum? Nightlife (Brannigans on a student night; top drawer)
And the worst? The accent or weather

Bobby Browns

48 Gas Street (0121) 643 2573

Not actually named after the man married to Whitney Houston, but that's their prerogative. Two floors of packed-out clubbing every night, every week all throughout the year. It's some credit to the management that they've managed to keep this place absolutely heaving without fail for over ten years, though what the secret to their success is we're not quite sure. Come the weekend, you can see 40-year old Colin, complete with middle-aged spread, eyeing up nubile 18-year old Louise from accounts. Before he has a chance to salivate down his shirt,

Hot tip

he comes bounding over, and asks him for a bottle of champagne. He agrees, hoping that Moet & Chandon might lead to a night of risqué wild abandon, but she glugs it down in one before joining the other girls in their hunt for the ideal sugar-daddy. Wednesdays sees a staggeringly popular student night, where tickets sell out weeks in advance. The only thing this night has in common with the others is the hordes of blaggers desperately trying to smooth their way past the fairly arbitrary door policy but you should know the rules by now. If your name's not John, you're definitely not coming in.

Bonds

Hampton Street, Hockley
(0121) 236 5503

Home to one of Brum's strictest dress codes, with the style squad patrolling up and down the queue rooting out unsuitable shirts, skirts, shoes and hairstyles, which leaves about half a dozen people in the queue. This sets the tone for the night – it's so imaged, that girls carry cordless hair tongs in their handbags for hourly chic check-ups. Seriously. The club's nothing special – one long room with a dancefloor sandwiched in between the seating area. But it's that pretentious tone of exclusivity which drives some of Birmingham's finest nights – at least in terms of music. Moneypenny's and Fuel are two nights famous country-wide, and behind the hype lie some cracking DJs and storming sets.

Code

Heath Mill Lane, Digbeth
(0121) 693 2633

Birmingham's latest addition to the club scene, and they've done a mighty fine job. Decades of club culture knowledge has been poured in from around the world to form this contender for the best venue country-wide. With a nigh-on perfect sound and lighting set and, without wishing to go over-the-top and kiss their nethers too much, a feel that's just 'right' about the whole venue. Balcony and seating overlook the main dancefloor with stages at both ends, but the club itself is a well-designed shell for the host of massive nights held here. The legendary Gods Kitchen, a night of hard house which can do absolutely no wrong, has recently upped sticks and taken root at Code on Fridays, bringing with it storming sets of big-name DJs (Tall Paul, Paul Oakenfold, Judge Jules, etc) with Lisa Lashes in residence, and, and, and oh God it's good. Babooshka on a Saturday is more your uplifting vocal house, now with Joey Negro in residence. Other nights vary – currently Sunday is Polysexual, and Wednesdays see a completely different but none-the-less brilliant cheese extravaganza, but these change so often your best bet is to check itchybirmingham.co.uk for more.

DNA
John Bright Street   (0845) 600 8007

Impressive-sized venue for an impressive-looking club. A balcony overlooks events, so you can check out the great big messy dancefloor on the ground where the uncoordinated bounce off one another, and for those who can dance without injuring someone, there's a stage. You can blag your way into the luxurious leather-seated VIP lounge or make do with the

Star Trek-esque Sky bar which hovers lik a spaceship above the crowd below, full complete with a vomit-inducing Perspe floor. There's even communal sinks, sure ly the precursor to communal toilets à Ally McBeal. As a venue, it's mighty fine whether you'll actually have a good tim or not depends entirely on the nigh Check itchybirmingham.co.uk for details

Dome II
Smallbrook Queensway

The mainstay of Birmingham tack ha now closed – for good. Police shut th place down after violence over-ruled th club. They tried to put up a fence to sto revellers chucking each other into th oncoming traffic but to no avail. Rumou had it that Zanzibar were trying to bu the place and take over but no chance the council has declared that this plac will never, ever open up as a club agai As defunct as the Millennium Dome.

The Hush
55 Station Street (0121) 242 6607
07939 954592 for membership details

The after hours party place for thos with membership. The place exudes coc and has seen just about every face i clubland drop by at some point or othe

Flick through the papers

here's no alcohol, but three bars for soft drinks, split over two floors – upstairs a bit more laid back, downstairs loud and bangin'. Loads of clubs host after-hour events here, so it does depend largely on the night – but suffice to say it's usually buzzing right up until closing, with an energetic crowd showing no signs of slowing down. Where do they get their energy from? Ahem.

The Glee Club

Arcadian Street, Hurst Street
0121) 242 6607

The only dedicated comedy club in Birmingham, but nevertheless it's a perfect-sized venue for all kinds of comedy. Intimate venue usually with make-shift, tacky but amusing discos after the shows keeping it going 'til 2am. Obviously only ever as good as the comedy, and I've seen some of the best and the most cringe-making death-on-stage shockers all in one night. Check chybirmingham.co.uk for details.

Flares

John Bright Street (0121) 616 7871

Two floors of 70s every bloody night. Stag and hen parties are well-catered for here, with crowds that are often old enough to remember 'It's Raining Men!' the first time around. Just let it go...

Liberty's

84 Hagley Road, Edgbaston
0121) 454 4444

Tucked away from all the action in town is the 'exclusive' Liberty's. When men are

past largin' it on Broad Street, they disappear for ten years and then don their jackets and return to Liberty's, armed with suave chat-up lines, money and a desperate urge to find a girl young and pretty enough to succumb to their worldly ways. And you thought that twinkle in your father's eye had something to do with your mother... Quite plush inside, complete with corridors of mirrors and velvet seating. There's nothing quite like it anywhere else in Birmingham. Or the UK for that matter.

McCluskys

53 Smallbrook Queensway
(0121) 616 3939

"Scarper, McClusky's coming!", screamed Zammo on Grange Hill. And if he lived in Brum, he'd still be saying the same thing. This gruesome American-themed chain has landed in our burgeoning bar area, and what a shocker. Usually, you associate metal detectors with your airports, but this is no holiday destination. Oh no – wth three floors of 'themed fun', and a 'restaurant' upstairs serving stringy burgers for twice their normal price, you'll know you're booked on the wrong flight. There's a dance floor of sorts on the ground floor, and a balcony that overlooks the mayhem and Elvis statues. Always packed, with a crowd that cockily assumes you most definitely are "lookin' at my bird". As the cast of Grange Hill would tell you, just say no.

Moseley Dance Centre
572-574 Moseley Road (0121) 449 0779

If ever you've got visitors to this fine city, then don't ever, ever take them here, as it'll only go to confirm all their suspicions of the city as a backward hell-water. In PR speak it's an awe-inspiringly airy venue with a dedicated food hall, dance stage and a happy, fun-loving crowd. So not a tatty church hall with Brian's disco box at one end and a staggeringly pissed up crowd of Moseley reprobates then, no? This place is so shamefully shit that it's quite good. It really is one big hall, complete with school chairs and tables laid out on the side as a 'chill out' area, and a mixture of 70s or 80s cheese depending on the night. The food hall is the school canteen, with staff like your favourite dinner-ladies, dishing up a few extra chips in return for cheeky banter. Full of those in Moseley who frankly can't be arsed to get dressed up, or just get dressed to go into town. Image is nothing, glasses are plastic, drinks are dirt cheap. Filthy fun.

Mustard
100 Watson Road, Star City
(0121) 327 2625

Another new addition to Birmingham' club scene, but it's a little too early to say what kind of impact it's going to make. Set in the heart of Star City, a multi-million pound entertainment complex, it's not going to have an easy ride. Just off the M6 for starters, and set amongst a multi-screen cinema and a tenpin bowling alley suggests that this could be a tacky affair of Dome-like proportions. Check itchybirmingham.co.uk for the latest news and reviews.

Hand book

──── ITCHY INFO ────

What:
[HARD HOUSE NIGHT]

With:
[LATE CLOSING]

Near where:
[TOWN CENTRE]

*SEARCH

OPTIONS   BACK

**What you want
when you need it
club info on the move
wap.itchybirmingham.co.uk**

The Que Club

**Central Hall, 212 Corporation Street
(0121) 212 0550**

Probably one of Birmingham's largest dance arenas and definitely one of the best, The Que Club boasts to be 'The House of the Techno Gods, where the infectious grooves will make your booties move'. Obviously. It specializes in all-nighters at the weekend, ranging from the renowned Sundissential to Atomic Jam. With four separate rooms you can usually find something to your taste, with big-name DJs playing techno, under-ground house, drum'n'bass and hip hop often on the same night. The main room is absolutely massive, literally the size of a church, and the tiered seating around the

top means that after dancing your nuts off, you can relax and soak up the electric atmosphere. No dress code, price s ranges from £10-£15, but it's better to buy your ticket in advance as it often sells out. If you want to thrash out a week's worth of frustration on the dance floor 'til 6am, this is the place to go. Alternatively if you want cheapness and cheese, there's also a student night on Mondays.

Ronnie Scotts

258 Broad Street (0121) 643 4525

The back of the venue houses the real Ronnie Scott's jazz club – for years, the only place in Brum with a 2am licence. They've been attracting a steady stream of quality jazz and blues acts for years, and they don't show any signs of letting up. There are rows and rows of tables facing the small dancefloor and stage, and

an atmosphere as lively as the band makes it. Obviously that's pretty hit and miss, but every time we've been here, the crowd were up on their feet getting stuck in. Food's a big part of the 'experience' – as are office parties. Do expect to see a few people your parents age hanging around, but there's a surprising absence of beard-stroking polo-necks, so you're probably best leaving the 'Jazz? Nice' gags at home.

The Sanctuary

Digbeth High Street (0121) 246 1010

This split-level club covers three rooms including a massive one, a chill out area and another room serving up different tunes from the main playlist. As with Code, the place really is just a shell (a red shell) for the variety of nights served up – a mixture of dance and indie. Despite losing Gods Kitchen on a Friday, they've replaced it with a serious con-

tender Hard House Heaven – matching God's exuberance and buzz as if it had never left the place. Saturday's R a m s h a c k l e moved off to the Academy, but S u p e r c h a r g e r have stepped in with an indie and big-beat extrava- ganza. Student

nights on Monday are still as popular and cheap as ever and all-in-all, though it's been a tumultuous few months for the club, they're still as strong and fresh as

before, bringing in new nights and new sounds into Birmingham's clubland.

Snobs

30 Paradise Circle, Queensway (0121) 643 5551

If you're over the age of, I dunno, about 22, this place may not hold out much attraction. But for the rest, this is the grungiest, moshiest pit of indie noise you'll find in Birmingham. This place hasn't seen an obvious refurb in years, but it doesn't matter, because the atmosphere brings it up to speed every night. Three bars, with two sandwiching the main dancefloor, and another smaller alternative room with a different playlist, housing an odd-looking circular bar. Old indie classics mix with modern, with every self-respecting indie kid clambering onto the podiums to show 'em all how it's done. Cheap, unadulterated teen-bopper fun. Absolutely no dress code whatsoever, though if you turn up in a suit they might need some convincing that you know what you're in for.

Take a leaf out of our book

Steering Wheel

Wrottesley St (0121) 666 6799

Another metal detector at the door affair, but this place has cleaned up its act of late, and is now home to some of the best dance nights in the West Midlands. The downstairs part of the club is mainly garage, but the place kicks into second gear upstairs in the house room. Surely has to be the only club that makes you pay twice for the privilege – once to get into the main room, and again to get upstairs. Double entry used to be common here as it was formerly home to Legs 11 (now round the corner), but that's no reason to carry on the theme. The crowd is as per any decent dance venue – energetic, glam and here for the 'choons.

Surfer's Paradise

Broad Street, underneath Walkabout (0121) 632 5712

Surfer's these days must be pretty hard up if this is their idea of paradise. This used to be a no-nonsense cheesy club playing anthemic tunes to a lashed-up crowd who'd dance the lambada without

a trace of irony. It still is, but the male to female ratio has tipped in a nasty way to the point where skirts are a novelty. Started to get a bit moody of late, and they can't find glass-collector staff in here for love nor money. Wonder why? Fingers crossed the bouncers will start cracking down on the crowd and get this place back on form. Inside it really is nothing special, nor big with seating surrounding the one main dance floor, and little else. There's still a few sports TV screens keeping the Walkabout theme through the place, but you can't help feeling you should be somewhere else.

Tower Ballroom

Reservoir Road, Edgbaston (0121) 454 0107

Ballrooms conjure up images of sweeping majestic affairs with finely-dressed crowds and high culture. The Tower has redefined the whole of that with a 'mature' crowd in 'basic' settings with 'down-to-earth' music and... look, if you're into the Tower, you'll have heard of it already. If not, you've got plenty of years yet before the need will strike you. Best

clubs

times for the Tower are the special events such as gigs and live fights (Thai-boxing championships most recently).

The Venue

Branston St, Hockley (0121) 636 6362

On the plus side, it's a dark urban ware-house, keeping it real with solid tunes and non-commerical cool. But then, in the cold light of day, the Venue really isn't anything special – a hastily converted fac-tory outlet with concrete walls, minimal seating and a few lights. You're here for the music, and the music only, and that depends entirely on the night. The only consistent theme is a rampant hatred of all things charty and populist.

XLs

Auchinleck Square, Five Ways (0121) 643 9433

Squashed in between a shopping centre and the Zig Zag strip joint is the oddest club in the city. You'll only know of it's existence by the sight of flapping combat trousers or long leather boots rushing past you on Broad Street, accompanied by the clinking of metal facial piercings. Home to rock of all descriptions, from your Fugazi to the Foo Fighters. There's three rooms – one is 'classic rock', remi-niscent of those ads on MTV, full of rock-ers who refuse to throw out those PVC jeans and black eyeliner. The place is one big mass of hair moshing to old glam, sleaze and classic rrrock which you'd forgotten ever existed. If that all proves a

bit much, there's an indie room for more modern, slightly mellower tunes. Glamorous it isn't, but these places aren't supposed to be – put simply, if you're into the scene, you'll find no better.

Zanzibar

Hurst Street (0121) 643 4715

Well you've got to thank them for knock-ing through into Central Park – they've done us all a favour. Zanzibar is a no-non-sense cheesy-type superclub, just as pre-vious incarnations as Ritzy's and Pulse were. Labyrinthine inside, with four differ-ent rooms (not always all open) varying from one that looks like a cave to a more clubby backroom. There's no pretensions about a place like this – nor the crowd – and for nights on the big session that'll end with stinging hangovers, come here and you'll be greeted with open arms car-rying a fag in one hand and a bottle of some funny-coloured alcopop in the other. This year they're beginning a selec-tion of live music events too, from tribute bands to the real thing. Sounds promising – check itchybirmingham.co.uk for more.

itchycities...

www.itchycity.co.uk

club listings

	Club	Night	Door tax	Hours	Comments
MON	Academy	Pump (student night)	£2.50 in advance, £3 on the door	9-2am	
	Bakers	Student night	£1.50 B4 10.30pm, £2.50 B4 11.30pm	2am	Chart anthems
	Circo Bar	Melange (funk, groove)	Free	2am	
	Mustard	Soul & Jazz	£2 entrance	8-12 midnight	
	Snobs	Slushpuppy (funky, indie)	£1.50 B4 10.30, £2 after	9.30-2am	DC: Relaxed
	Zanzibar	60s to chart pop	Free B4 10.30, then £3	8.30-2am	DC: Smart casual dress, no blue denim or trainers
TUES	Miss Moneypenny's	R&B Experience	Free	9-11	DC: Smart casual
	Mustard	One Dollar (club classic and funky house)	£2	8-2am	Most drinks £1
	Zanzibar	60s to chart pop	Free B4 10.30, then £3	8.30-2am	DC: Smart casual dress, no blue denim or trainers
WED	Bakers	Congress (house classics from 90-98)	Free B4 11.30, £3 after	10pm-2am	DC: Urban clubwear but no trainers (eh?!)
	Bar 260	Congress (house)	£3 B4 11, £5 after	10-3am	DC: No trainers
	Bobby Browns	Student	£3 with NUS	9-2am	
	Circo	Cocoa (Latin beats)	Free	9-2am	DC: Relaxed Latin flavour
	DNA	Code Red (student night)	£3 NUS, £4 others	9-2.30am	DC: Relaxed
	Liberty's	Commercial Dance	Free B4 9.30 and for ladies all night, £6 gents	10.30-2am	
	Medicine Bar	Lupa (beats and breaks, 1st Wed of month)	Free	9-2am	DC: Relaxed
	Mustard	Big Cheese	£2	8-2am	all draughts £1 a pint. Buses from uni's
	Snobs	Big Wednesday (indie, mod and soul)	Cheap	10-2am	
	Sobar Bar	Bish Bash Bong (world music)	Free	9-2.30am	DC: Relaxed
	Zanzibar	60s to chart pop	Free B4 10.30, then £3	8.30-2am	DC: Smart casual dress, no blue denim or trainers
THU	Bobby Browns	Student	£3 with NUS	9-2am	
	DNA	Fizzy Pop (70s, 80s, 90s)	£2.50 NUS, £4.50 others	9-2am	DC: Smart casual. Buses from 'It's a Scream' pubs across city
	Liberty's	Commercial Dance	Free B4 9.30 in bar, £3 after	10.30-2am	DC: Smart casual
	Medicine Bar	Amplified (hip hop and funk)	Free	9-late	
	Miss Moneypenny's	Barefoot in the Head (funk, disco and hip hop)	Free	9-11	
	Mustard	Mine (garage)	£2 til 10.30, £3 after	8-2am	DC: No effort, no entry
	Stoodi Bakers	Spin (hard house)	£2.50 B4 10.	8-2am	DC: Urban
	Zanzibar	60s to chart pop	Free B4 10.30, then £3	8.30-2am	DC: Smart casual dress, no blue denim or trainers

Roll up

Club	Night	Door tax	Hours	Comments
Academy	Ramshackle (student indie and funk)	£4	10-3am	DC: Laid-back
Bakers	Horny (house)	£3 before 12, £5 after with flyer	10pm-4am	Residents - Stu Brookes
Bobby Browns		£6		DC: Smart
Code	Gods Kitchen (cutting edge hard/funky house)	£8 NUS, £9 members, £10 others	9.30-4am	DC: Glam and dressy
Liberty's	Commercial dance	Free B4 9.30, £8 after	10.30-2am	
Medicine Bar	Varies between house, reggae, DnB and funk	Free B4 9pm, £2 after	9-2am	DC: Relaxed (as ever)
Moseley Dance Centre	70s night	£5	10-2am	DC: Relaxed, though any thing goes
Mustard	Lovefunk (funky house)	£2 til 10.30, £3 after	8-2am	DC: No effort, no entry
Que Club	Atomic Jam (techno funk, beats, breaks, d n b)	£6 members, £8 B4 11 & NUS, £10 after/others	10-6am	Awesome night by anyone's standards
Snobs	Various nights, including Loaded. Indie-themed	£4	10-3am	DC: Relaxed
Steering Wheel	Sweet n Sexy (garage)	£5	10-4am	DC: "Smooth and sexy, no caps or trainers
Subway	Spacehopper (gay house)	£6 members, £7 non	9-3am	
Venue	Venue (house, US garage)	£8	10-6am	
Zanzibar	60s to chart pop	Free B4 10.30, then £3 'til 11, £5 after	8.30-2am	DC: Smart casual dress, no blue denim or trainers

Club	Night	Door tax	Hours	Comments
Academy	Blast! (grunge/indie)	£5	10-3am	DC: Laid-back
Bakers	Republica	£4 before 11, £6 after with flyer	10pm-4am	Residents Brent Cross, Ranier, Jimmy Hill
Bobby Browns		£7	9-3am	DC: Smart
Bonds	Miss Monepenny's	£10	9.30-3am	DC: Glam
Circo	Global Hi-Fi (jazz house	Free	9-2am	DC: Individual /hip hop)
Code	Babooshka (garage, hse)	£10 NUS, £11 members, £12 others	9.30-4am	DC: Chic
Medicine Bar	Alternates between DnB, breaks and beats and funk	Free B4 9pm, £2 after	9-2am	
Moseley Dance	80s night	£5	10-2am	DC: Relaxed, though anything goes
Mustard	Dance night	£2 til 10.30, £3 after	8-2am	DC: No effort, no entry
Que Club	Flashback (underground dance)	£15	10-6am	
Sanctuary	Broken Minds (DnB)	£3 B4 11.30pm		
Snobs	Various (indie-themed)	£5	10-3am	DC: Relaxed
Venue	Play House (deep house & US garage)	£9	10-6am	
Zanzibar	60s to chart pop and commercial dance	Free B4 10.30, then £3 'til 11, £5 after	8.30-2am	DC: Smart casual dress, no blue denim or trainers

For up-to-date information check

www.itchybirmingham.co.uk

All listings details are susceptible to change at short notice, and should therefore be used as a guide only.

gay
www.itchycity.co.uk

The UK's second city is renowned for being many things; the gay scene isn't one of them. There's still quite a lot going on – just past the main run of bars on Hurst Street lies a fair few venues and should be your main starting point, and take it from there. As a general rule, Broad Street should be avoided unless you're looking to take on the world.

Bars

Boots Bar
77 Wrenthamn Street (0121) 622 1414
Birmingham's answer to Amsterdam (in a gay way, rather than skunk-smoking). Dress code is denim, leather or skin, depending on your fancy. Covering a wide age span, this place is a must for those who like the darker side of the gay scene. So if you're sick to death of Abba medleys on constant loop while Gaynor wannabes prance around camping it up, you may have found your home. Music varies from the questionable to the shoddy.

Angel's
125-131 Hurst Street (0121) 622 4880
The owner Gareth seems to lead the scene with a series of promotions and events, often copied by other bars across the city. Right in the heart of the gay village, this place attracts a pre-club crowd, with the young 'uns at the weekend gearing up to the night ahead with loud and pumping dance tracks. There's an airy feel with large windows to pose through, and once the place packs out and the bar gets going, the windows steam up. DJs on the weekend, naturally.

board, mingling in this low-lit affair usually creating a vibrant atmosphere. So long as you stay, your entry fee won't be wasted, so the value of your night largely depends on the crowd it draws in – hit and miss.

Missing

48 Bromsgrove Street (0121) 622 3951

Fabulous entertainment, every night. This place camps it up more than a Carry On film with everything from karaoke to strippers, drag and live PA's. In the summer during the day they fling open the doors and stick seats outside to chill with a G&T and watch the passing trade.

Partners Bar

27-35 Hurst Street (0121) 622 4710

Another bar with its foot firmly in the camp side of entertainment, with a variety of acts nightly. Despite the down-at-heel exterior, inside it's quite cosy and intimate, providing a pleasant respite from the sticky heat of summer. Best thing about this place is your ability to make a grand entrance into the bar, giving everyone a chance to check you out and for you to suss the crowd before you enter.

Route 2

139-147 Hurst Street (0121) 622 3366

Major mixed feelings about this place as they charge to enter most nights; admittedly Thursday's quite a cheap affair, but as a rule the door tax seems a little sniffy. A happy mixture of ages across the

The Victoria

48 John Bright Street, (0121) 633 9439

Sitting at the back of the Alex is the Victoria, with a mixture of actors with their air-kissing graces and a fairly effeminate crowd (mixture of gay and straight). Being quite close to DNA, you could envisage it being a pre-club pub. Think again – two more opposite crowds are hard to imagine. Two floors and traditional décor.

The Fountain

102 Wrentham Street (0121) 622 1452

This pub/hotel has a long bar for watchful service and pool table. What's more, once you've had a few you can doss down here for the night at £30 for a single, or £45 for a double. The crowd is definitely older and more sedate than elsewhere in the gay village; less DKNY and GAP, more M&S and Millets.

Who are you exactly?
Lars, 28, travelling salesman from Norway
Travel far for a drink? Nope; the Village Inn does the job, and I'm staying upstairs
Experienced any of the clubs yet?
Nightingales was a beautifully crazy night
Less said the better. Do you like Brum? Yeah, all the places I've been to seem to have a cool continental feel
Anything bad about it? You Britons seem to drink far too much

The Fox
12 Lower Essex Street (0121) 622 1210
Beer garden / pool room / two bars
There are few places in Brum that cater for us lesbians specifically – most of us make do with mingling in with the other places. But hallelujah for The Fox, because it's specifically aimed at catering for those who are fonder of the fairer sex. Still a smattering of men paying a passing visit, but the largely warm and friendly atmosphere is formed through kinship. Huge beer garden for long summer evenings, a pool room and two bars.

The Wellington Hotel
72 Bristol Street
Actually more of a mixed bar on account of its position slightly out of the village.

But it's a traditional pub with bent leanings – work your way up to Bristol Street and keep your eye out for the rainbow flag.

The Village Inn
Gay Pub / Hotel
152 Hurst Street (0121) 622 4742
Beer garden & bar
Often overlooked by the younger crowd as being an old mans' pub but my word, nothing could be further from the truth. Cracking as a place to meet up with an eclectic gay crowd from all corners of the Midlands. The music's a big drawer here, with some of the best underground tunes on a garage tip keeping the crowd bouncing along. And yes, gay people like garage too.

The Jester
Horsefair, Holloway Circus
Round the corner from the gay village this tends to be pretty quiet. But a change is as good as a break – apparently – and this is different from the norm. It's a basement bar, so like Partners, ideal to get away from the heat in summer, and it's biggest feature is the roundness of the place with the bar slap bang in the

centre. You can see everyone and everyone can see you. Be afraid!

The White Swan
Sherlock Street/Hurst Street
(0121) 693 5042
With a happy hour from 2pm-7pm seven days a week, this place always draws in the punters. Beware, many a soul has popped in for a quick one and before they know it, it'll be getting late and they'll put their name down for karaokehoping that the next punter who walks through the door will be an A&R man, desperate to replace H from steps. Dream on boys.

Clubs

Subway City
27 Water Street, Old Snow Hill
(0121) 233 0310
Old Snow Hill
Green Room / Blue Room / Pink Room / Naff Caff
The club for dancing and mixing it up. It gets all too hot and sticky all too quickly but that's half the point. Music is hard and thumping, but there's plenty of chill out areas for respite, with the Naff Caff

which does exactly what is says on the door, to the exceedingly camp Pink Room, where you'll find Abba and Steps acted out by plastered queens – the idea is not to take it too seriously, and even the butchest of butch can be seen mouthing along to lyrics of Ms Gaynor and friends. Also home to strippers from time to time, though whether they're paid to appear or the fancy just takes 'em, no-one seems to know.

The Nightingale
Essex House, Kent Street, City Centre
(0121) 622 1718
The oldest gay club in Birmingham and most likely due for a refit soon if the committee can decide what colour the wooden floor should be. Still a member's club as it was before, but now they've gleaned a full licence, you can get in by paying just a bit extra. Packed out all weekend with three floors of happening tunes, this is the key gay venue in Brum. From time to time the main dancefloor pauses for some entertainment from the in-your-face strippers. Aired on Queer as Folk not so long ago, bringing the occasional straight dipping their toe into the gay scene, sometimes ending up with it being sucked!

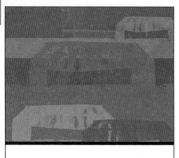

shopping
www.itchycity.co.uk

You may notice that Birmingham town centre currently looks like war-torn Sarajevo, with temporary roads and half-destroyed buildings. Grim as it looks, this is the city's much needed face-lift and multi-billion pound development involving a complete renovation of everything from the Bull Ring to the Rag Market, as well as the introduction of some of the finest high street shops. Everything is in a state of flux at present, so check itchybirmingham.co.uk for the latest details.

Incidentally, if you come across someone on the street asking you if you've ever wondered about the meaning of life, scarper. The Moonies are in force and are tireless in their campaign for new recruits. Moonies? Moomins more like...

Shopping Centres

Bull Ring Indoor Market Hall
Bull Ring (0121) 607 6000
If you can find it (right next to the Rotunda) in and amongst all the building work, you'll find loads, nearly 200 stalls with everything from clothes to seafood and fruit. It's undergoing a huge renovation like the whole of this area, so keep your eyes peeled for the latest developments.

Bull Ring Open Market
Bull Ring (0121) 303 0300
Right next to St Martin's church is the open market with a startling array of fresh food from around the world. Previously shunned by some for looking

a bit ropy, the food's actually some of the finest in the city but the grubby surroundings weren't. Again under serious redevelopment, which should be finished in early 2001.

City Plaza
47 Cannon Street (0121) 633 3969

Mon-Sat 8.30-6pm, Sun 10-5pm

A night out at a bar, smooth lines, several cocktails later and they're laughing at your jokes. You're in your element. A few cheeky innuendos and it's back to their house. Coffee, kiss and up to the bedroom. Clothes ripped off each other's backs, down to your keks. But what's that? Non-labelled underwear! You should be ashamed. The moment's gone, there's nothing you can do, but vow to stock up on designer gear for next time at City Plaza. For when image is everything, a place full of the more exclusive boutiques and outlets in Brum. Kitted out with a great big glass dome, a couple of cafes and a range of exclusive stores.

Jewellery Quarter
Hockley (0121) 554 3598

Where else can you find a place where history stands still and things are made as they always were, without any of your fancy machinery, gadgets and gubbins? Eh? It's rhetorical – there are plenty of places across the UK, but this is definitely one of the finest. Producing high quality, low cost jewellery of all descriptions. Ignore your H. Samuels and find the real masters of their trade across the hundreds of workshops in the area.

The Mailbox
Suffolk Street Queensway, Royal Mail Street (0121) 643 4080

Mon-Sat 10-6, rests 'til 11pm. Sun tbc.

One of the biggest, most expensive, most impressive shopping centres to open in the UK in ages. It used to be the old Royal Mail sorting office, but several million pounds later, it's Birmingham's new home for the swankiest of stores, restaurants, hotels and apartments, all set among landscaped squares, a slice of

contemporary art and waterside streets, bridges and piazzas. They've already submitted new roads to the A-Z, but will they change the face of Birmingham shopping? It's still early days yet, and at the time of going to print only a handful of shops were open, including Christian Lacroix, Emporio Armani and Ronit Zilkha (women's fashion for those not short of a few quid). But there's a whole host of places set to open in 2001, from

Harvey Nichols (in summer) to Hugo Boss, Descamps and Essensuals. They've already set the tone here – it will be the finest, most extravagant designer outlet in town. Combined with a number of bars and restaurants, it's well worth visiting often to find out what's new and what's going on. And if you were wondering about the roof-top canal-side apartments, forget it – all 200 are already let. Check itchybirmingham.co.uk for the latest details.

The Pallasades Shopping Centre
(0121) 633 3070
Mon-Sat 9-5.30, Thu ('til 7pm), Sun 11-5
Connected to New Street station is the ubiquitous Pallasades shopping centre – as much a part of the city as the Rotunda and UB40. Shops change hands here with alarming rates, but there's over 80 different stores at present, so you're fairly certain to find something of interest. Less clothes, more toys, phones, electrics and books orientated.

Merry Hill Centre
Brierley Hill, West Midlands
(01384) 481141
Mon-Fri 10-8 (Thu 9pm, Sat 9-7, Sun 11-5. OK, not exactly on the doorstep, but this is an out-of-town shopping centre well worth taking a look at. 200 stores under one roof with free parking means that if you're not keen on traipsing round for the day you can theoretically be in and out before you can say "insufficient funds". Masses of high street names here, and little in the way of boutiques. Also home to a cinema, obviously – this is a "one-stop shopping and entertainment extravaganza" don't you know?

Paradise Forum
Paradise Place
Most people fly through here on the way to Broad Street, but a couple of little jewellery boutiques and cafes make it a pleasant enough stop-off point after a day's manic shopping.

Pavilions Shopping Centre
38 High Street (0121) 631 4121
Mon-Fri 9.30-6 (7pm Thu), Sat 9-6, Sun 11-7
One of the first shopping centres in Brum back in the 80s, when the glass lift was met with gasps of amazement. Nowadays, there's nothing out of the ordinary here, but it serves up a respectable number of high street shops, from Next to Laura Ashley, HMV to Marks & Spencer. There's

stacks of gift shops full of stuff that you'd never dream of buying for yourself – candlewax pens and plastic goldfish for starters. At the top of the centre is the food court, with nine different kiosks serving up a reasonable range of cuisine. Well, cuisine in some cases, monstrously overpriced paltry offerings in others. Best bet is to hover around the ever-present queues and inspect passing shoppers' plates to see what they're getting.

Priory Square Shopping Centre
Priory Walk

Alongside the open air market you'll find Argos (the most unhelpful staff in the whole city), Virgin and Oasis. But for real bargains, try the surrounding open-air market with enough jeans, leather coats, watches and dodgy electricals to keep Arthur Daley in business for a lifetime. Haggling will always be met with an incredulous "Behave!", but usually works. Jewel in the crown round here is Oasis, a range of self-contained independent stores, selling everything from jewellery to leather-jackets. You can spend hours in

here just wandering round, collecting smoking gear, novelty lighters and piercings on the way.

The (Temporary) Rag Market
Currently at Edgbaston Street
(opp. Hurst Street) Thu, Fri, Sat

Hold the front page – the world famous Rag Market is about to reopen in a spanking new building. Selling just about every bargain you can possibly imagine, from unbelievably cheap clothes to car stereos to air freshner to cactus plants. There's not a lot you can't find if you look hard enough, and with it's much-needed new home, it'll be able to shrug off its previous shonky image. Hopefully...

▮ Department stores

Surprisingly for a city of this size, department stores are in extremely short supply. The ubiquitous yet shoddy C&A was just closing as this went to print, but it's no great loss – leaving the big three still standing.

shopping

BHS

6-9 New Street (0121) 643 8541

You should know what to expect by now, with everything from homeware to clothing, all made with the British stamp of quality. Cue bargain hunting old folk and sulky eleven year old girls trying to persuade their mums' that belt-like mini skirts are regulation school wear.

Marks & Spencer

42 High Street (0121) 643 4511

Should need no introduction. Contains a vast food hall too for purchasing that romantic dinner for two that you cooked yourself, honest.

Rackhams

Corporation Street (0121) 236 3333

Blow your pocket money, bonus or year's salary here, easily. Catering to the plusher end of Birmingham's shoppers, this place has everything a large department store should have, from perfume counters to designer-label gear at designer-label prices. Even in the sales, prices only seem to come down to standard high street mark-ups, but that's the price you pay for fashion...

Cult Clothing

29/30 Stephenson Street
(0121) 643 1051

Skater kids and accountants trying to look cool all meet in freestyle urban streetwear.

Diesel

8-9 Lower Temple Street
(0121) 632 5575

Ever popular Italian designer jeans and urban streetwear.

Gap

40 New Street (0121) 633 0644

Infuriating adverts and terrifyingly friendly staff. But a good starting point for wardrobe basics.

Marks & Spencer

4 High Street (0121) 643 4511

MK1

Unit 47 The Pallasades / 57 High Street
(0121) 633 8808 / 543 4363

Never been one to attract the glitterati, but for the cheapest, cheapest clothes known to man you'll be hard pushed to find better. T-shirts for a quid but style is not an optional extra.

Next

Pavilions, 38 High Street
(0121) 631 3600

Principles

18 New Street (0121) 243 0455

Reiss

32 New Street (0121) 632 6054
Probably the best menswear shop in Birmingham, now with a women's section too. Stylish, expensive but well-made.

River Island

70 High Street (0121) 236 1028

Top Shop/Top Man

74-75 High Street (0121) 643 0348
The girls see this place as a quick fix to every Friday night outfit dilemma, though the same can't really be said about the men's gear, ranging from the innocuous to the tacky.

Clothes – men's

Aquascutum

Rackhams, Temple Row
(0121) 236 9442
Pricey designer-ish gear ranging from the cool to the over-branded.

Austin Reed

4 North Walk, The Pallasades
(0121) 643 0072
Jeeves and Wooster would be in their element...

Capolito Roma

City Plaza, Cannon Street
(0121) 633 4373

Ciro Cittero

60 Corporation Street (0121) 236 6267

High & Mighty

72-74 Smallbrook Queensway
(0121) 543 1940
A euphemism for the tall, the wide or the oddly-shaped, but stylish nonetheless.

Jaeger Man

Rackams, 35 Temple Row
(0121) 236 5093
Like the female equivalent, for the more discerning dresser with discerning tastes and a full wallet.

Kensington Freak

145 New Street, 42a New Street
(0121) 643 9448/643 1160
Bit townie, but the odd decent garment here and there.

Limeys

14 Stephenson Street (0121) 643 3227
High fashion with designer labels and prices to match.

Slater Menswear

3 Cannon Street (0121) 633 3855
A massive store tucked away on Cannon Street featuring a whole variety of common labels at knock-down prices. Best for suits and shirts, though you can find the odd casual bargain.

The Suit Co

**Pavilions, 38 High Street
(0121) 631 1218**
Suits, obviously, plus the odd bit of casual gear

Timberland

11-14 Cannon Street (0121) 633 9349

Clothes – women's

Ann Harvey

**Pavilions, 38 High Street
(0121) 643 3250**

Autograph

15 Ethel Street (0121) 643 3989
From the classic designers to the latest

street brands. An independent retailer with an extraordinary collection of the hip, the sassy and the downright outrageous.

Dorothy Perkins

50-54 High Street (0121) 643 2967

Etam

23 New Street (0121) 643 2800
Hard times call for hard measures, and shopping in Etam is usually the last resort. Everything you never knew you wanted at prices that you'd be pushed to complain about.

Evans

**Pavilions, 38 High Street
(0121) 631 4755**
Catering for the larger woman in style.

Flannels

**14 Lower Temple Street
(0121) 633 4154**
More exciting than the image of a soggy flannel may suggest – Gucci, Prada, Jil Sander etc. Not one for munters.

French Connection

39-40 Cannon Street (0121) 633 9304
Full of clothes emblazoned with "fcuk", a fcuking overused gag, ho ho.

Name, age and occupation?
Roxanne, 22, Insurance agent

Guaranteed good night out?
Stoodi Bakers for a good binge

Best shop? Top Shop

Favourite place for food? Las Iguanas (love the atmosphere)

And for clubbing? The Sanctuary every time

Brum's best point? The people!

And worst? We need more bars

Giant

Corporation Street (0121) 212 3488

Good fashionable gear at the pricier end of the high street market. They change their range every three months

Hobbs (Marilyn Anselm)

85 Temple Row, 3rd floor in Rackhams
(0121) 233 0773

Classic, understated clothes for the older shopper.

Jaeger

11 City Plaza Cannon Street / 35
Temple Row (0121) 633 4381 / 236 6372

Stylish, svelte and attractive, and that's just the staff. For times when looking simply good isn't enough...

Jeffrey Rogers

Pavilions, 38 High Street
(0121) 643 4536

Simple, averagely priced clothes with a section for the bigger-framed among us.

Jigsaw

Cannon Street, Caxtongate
(0121) 633 9475

Bold and brassy, just like its range of clothes. One of the best high-quality high street shops around.

Jones Bootmaker

122 New Street, Unit 3 The Burlington
(0121) 643 0643

Every kind of shoe for affluent shoppers of all ages.

 Find the nearest cash points on your phone
wap.itchybirmingham.co.uk

Karen Millen
Unit 6 The Burlington, New Street
(0121) 643 5020
One of the most heavily popular stores on the whole high street, full of wide-eyed and delirious umming and ahhing over the latest suits and dresses. Not especially well-made, but infinitely stylish.

La Senza
Pavilions, 38 High Street
(0121) 643 2228

Laura Ashley
Pavilions, 38 High Street
(0121) 633 8778
Your RS teacher probably shops here, with floral designs and gaudy colours to frighten small children.

Mexx
41 High Street (0121) 643 7824
Understated clean-lines, where brand isn't as important as style.

Miss Selfridge
79 High Street (0121) 643 4417

Treat with caution if you're an enormously huge person (in Miss Selfridge world this constitutes anyone over a size ten) the changing rooms are a living hell- 15 year old stick insects whinging about having no boobs. Give it a rest.

Monsoon
Pavilions, 38 High Street / City Plaza Cannon Street
(0121) 643 0019/643 1927
For the older woman, full of exotic clothes with brightly styled fabrics, from the plain and simple to oriental.

New Look
51 The Pallasades (0121) 632 5589
Cheap and effective high fashion for serious bargain hunters. It's also worth noting that it's officially cool to buy stuff from New Look and publically brag about how cheap it was. If it's good enough for Natalie Appleton...

Next
138 New Street (0121) 631 3113

www.itchybirmingham.co.uk

Nicholls Exclusive Clothing
1 Temple Row (0121) 687 5555
A range of the most exclusive labels in town, including D&G, Versace, Hugo Boss and Alexander McQueen.

Oasis
125 New Street (0121) 643 2770
Keeping a watchful eye on the latest fashions, Oasis offer the latest styles at reasonable prices. Mainly casual clothes, ranging from stuff you could get away with at work (jackets) to stuff that'd probably get you the sack (gold lame bikinis anyone?). Not to be confused with the department store of the same name.

Red or Dead
**14 Caxton Gate, Cannon Street
(0121) 631 2064**
With their own take on High Street fashions, Red provide high-quality own-label clobber for the discerning dresser, and the odd off-the-wall number.

Nostalgia & Comics Ltd
**14-16 Smallbrook Queensway
(0121) 643 0143**
Those nostalgic for the old comics and sci-fi publications of yester-year will be in their element. And if you're really desperate for presents, how does a Dalek grab you?

Waterstone's
**Aston Uni Branch, 12 Gosta Green
(0121) 359 3242
24 High Street (0121) 633 4353
128 New Street (0121) 631 4333**

The Works
**137 New St B2 4NS (0121) 643 3092
8 Pallasades B2 4XA (0121) 643 2877**

W H Smith
29 Union Street (0121) 631 3303

Hard to Find Records
**10 Upper Gough Street
(0121) 643 5292**
Dance and house. Apparently the staff can sometimes get a bit sniffy, but who cares? You're looking for hard to find records aren't you? If they're dance/house affairs, you'll do no better.

HMV
**Pavilions, 38 High Street
(0121) 643 2177**

Magpie Records
363 Bristol Road South (0121) 476 7255
Why did the lion get lost? Coz jungle is masseev. And so's their collection.

Plastic Factory
**183 Corporation Street
(0121) 233 2967**
A whole mish-mash of music, with a leaning towards punk, new wave and psychedelia. Lots of second-hand records, together with a special category of music called 'Difficult'.

Swordfish Records
14 Temple Street (0121) 633 4859
Unbelievably popular independent, specialising in dance and indie. Home to all kinds of CDs and vinyl far cheaper than the high street, with staff a hell of a lot more knowledgeable and friendly too. Also the place in Brum to pick up flyers and book tickets for the cooler events in the city. Not particularly big, but well worth a visit.

Tempest
83 Bull Street (0121) 236 9170
House and garage specialists, with an almost bouncer-like air about the staff unless you know your tunes. Indie section downstairs, as well as a vast range of concert tickets.

Tower Records
5 Corporation Street (0121) 616 2677
Stocks an impressive array of music in the usual shopper-friendly style. Staff aren't as knowledgeable as some of the independents, but always friendly and happy to help where they can.

Vinyl Matters
8 Lower Severn Street (0121) 687 2772
For all that's house and dance.

Virgin
98 Corporation Street (0121) 236 2523

CORKER

RIZLA+WARE

For the full Rizlaware range just visit www.rizla.com or call 07000 749527

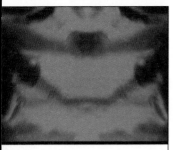

entertainment

www.itchycity.co.uk

There are a stack of cinema and bowling alleys across the city, but none so big nor so glamourous as **Star City** (contact 0870 844 6600 for details). It's a brave Vegas-inspired multi-million pound entertainment complex where they've gone to town on everything. They obviously run the risk that it'll look dated in a couple of years, but in the meantime you can't fail to be impressed by the flashing lights and glitzy, chintzy surroundings. There's a 30-screen cinema covering everything from the usual Hollywood blockbusters to arthouse and Bollywood classics – in short, something for every taste. And that's not all. There's a 24-lane **MegaBowl**, and a host of restaurants and bars, including **Bar Censsa**, **De:Alto** and **Nando's**, to name but a few. There's even a great big club called **Mustard** inside the place as if that weren't enough. It's still a new venture, and the key to its success will be to see if the outlets can develop personalities of their own rather than feeling like one big corporate mish-mash. Time will tell...

Five Ways Leisure Centre has also made an impressive crash into the entertainment scene. It's not yet complete, but

the first phase with a 12-screen cinema (with stadium-style seating) and café bar is now complete. The most impressive thing about the complex is **Tiger Tiger** next door – see Bar section.

Odeon Cinema
New Street 0870 505 0007
Adults £4.50
NUS £3.50

UGC Cinema Arcadian Centre
Hurst Street 0870 155 5177
Adults £5.00
NUS £3.50

UGC Cinema Five Ways Leisure Park
Broad Street, Five Ways 0870 907 0723
Adults £5.00
NUS £3.50

0870 907 0726
Rubery

Warner Village Cinemas Star City
Watson Road, Nechells (0121) 326 0246
Adults £5.50
NUS £4.00
30 Screens

Theatres

Alexandra Theatre
Suffolk Street Queensway 0870 6077533
Just a short hop from New Street station is the Alex, home to a number of pro-

ductions hot from the West End. The biggest draw here is the D'Oyly Carte Opera company, for the infamous Gilbert and Sullivan operas. Fa-la-la-li...

Birmingham Hippodrome
Hurst Street (0121) 689 3000
(under major redevelopment opening Sep 2001)

Birmingham Repertory Theatre
Centenary Square, Broad Street (0121) 236 4455
Harking back to 1913, this is Birmingham's most critically acclaimed theatre and has seen the likes of Laurence Olivier and Albert Finney gracing its boards. There are two stages – one 900-seat Main House for the mainstream performances, and a smaller 140-seat Studio for the more experimental and cutting edge productions. Seats start at around a fiver, and are rarely more expensive than £15.

Crescent Theatre
Brindleyplace, Broad Street (0121) 643 5858
This is one place in Birmingham that des-

perately needs support. It's a purpose-built theatre housing a main theatre, together with tons of modern facilities (workshops, rehearsal rooms, galleries etc) and it's home to its own amateur theatre company. For a list of forthcoming productions, check itchybirmingham.co.uk for details.

■ Galleries and Museums

Midlands Art Centre (Mac)
Cannon Hill Park (0121) 440 4221
Mon-Sun 9-11pm
This place deserves a couple of pages all to itself, but we don't have room, so here's the abbreviated version. Not just a gallery, theatre, cinema, but a centre of excellence for the arts in the city. Usually the heart of a city-centre park sees little more than glue-sniffing and spliff-smoking kids, but the Mac has changed all that. Set in the resplendent Cannon Hill park, this is the key focus for arts in the city. With over half a million visitors every year, they cater for just about everything – from theatre, to cinema (the stuff you won't find at the multiplex), to dance and comedy. There are so many events here it's hard to catch up (though we'll be covering them all at itchybirmingham.co.uk) – suffice to say, if you're after a dose of culture, whether it be a Spanish class or life painting classes, you're bound to find something of interest here. Home to a café restaurant, bar and bookshop too.

Barber Institute
The University of Birmingham
Edgbaston (0121) 414 7333
This resplendent building is home to 20th century art of all descriptions. If nothing else, the atmosphere is chilled and thought-provoking, with numerous highly-respected exhibitions featuring all year round. Highly respected in art circles, but go for a visit and make up your own mind.

Birmingham Museum & Art Gallery
Chamberlain Square (0121) 303 2834
Mon-Sat 10-5 (10.30 Fri), Sun 12.30-5. Free, but make a donation and don't be pikey.
An impressive collection of art, ranging from a great deal of pre-Raphaelite paintings to some more modern works, together with items of interest from across the ages. Usually plays host to a few exhibitions – ring for details.

Ikon Gallery
1 Oozells Square, Brindleyplace
(0121) 248 0708
Tue-Sun 11-6, closed Mondays except Bank Holidays. Free
So cool, even the address has kudos. This is a two-floored gallery with 440 square metres of space, housing constantly changing exhibitions and installations. A lot more interactive and often surreal than some of Brum's other more staid counterparts, the Ikon displays contemporary art at its finest across a mixed bag of media – sometimes photography, sometimes paintings but more often than not a mixture of sound, video, sculpture and just about any other format you can think of. Highly recommended.

Museum of the Jewellery Quarter
Vyse Street, Hockley (0121) 554 3598
Mon-Fri 10-4pm, Sat 11-5pm
Adult £2.50, NUS £2.00
Showing you how they made jewellery 200 years ago. Fascinating as it is, you can't help noticing that actually not a lot's changed over the years. So, in a sense, it isn't really a museum, though if you visit it in around 30 odd years, you might be in luck.

The Glee Club
The Arcadian Centre, Hurst Street
(0121) 693 2248
Comedy nights Thu-Sat all year.
Student nights Oct-Mar on Wednesdays
Discos on Fri/Sat nights also.
It's surprising that the UK's second city doesn't have more in the way of comedy, but of what there is, it's done well. For years, we were missed off the comedy circuit but now this has become an essential stop for everyone from well-known faces to the up and coming. A top night out.

Sports and Leisure

Ackers Trust
Golden Hillock Road, Small Heath
(0121) 772 5111
Mon 1-10pm, Tue-Fri 10-10pm, Sat-Sun 10-6pm
Snowboard club every Thurs 3hrs for £10
If hurtling down a fibre-glass mountain and bone-crunchingly painful falls do it for you, then the Ackers Trust dry ski slope may be right up your street. If not, there's just about every other outdoor activity available too, including climbing, abseiling, canoeing, orienteering and caving.

Aston Villa Football Club
Villa Park (0121) 327 2299
Aston Villa
Tickets from £15 (concessions £5)
Villa, based at the impressive Villa Park,

have been an enigma team for the last few years with a fluctuating league and cup form which has left the future of manager John Gregory in doubt. However a recent run of good results has ensured that "Deadly" Doug Ellis will be keeping the P45 tucked away – for the time being. Boasting a squad which includes England internationals Gareth Southgate, David James, Gareth Barry, Paul Merson and Steve Stone, Villa have failed to live up to expectations and this has been reflected through falling gates as disgruntled fans hit the clubs where it hurts the most. However the recent capture of the club's record signing, Juan Pablo Angel may just give the fans something to cheer about – or he could be another Savo or Stan.

Name, age and occupation?
Sally, 24, Recruitment consultant
Where do you dress? H&M or Flannels when I'm feeling flush
Best for a cheeky half? Mellow or Casa
And then to shake it down? Medicine Bar at the weekends – storming sets!
How about a meal? Bits'n'Pizza. The name's cack, but it's decent in there
Brum. What's good? Love the nightlife
And what's not? Hate the chain bars

Birmingham City Football Club
St Andrews Road (0121) 772 0101
Tickets from £16 (concessions £8)
After a slow start to the season Birmingham City FC are now beginning to demonstrate the form that has seen them progress from 1st division pretenders to genuine promotion contenders. The impressive St Andrews stadium mirrors the potential of the club and players who under the only female football managing director, Karen Brady and outspoken manager Trevor Francis, have ensured that the West Midlands may well have two teams competing in the Premiership next season. I know we should be impartial, but Christ, let's hope so.

West Bromwich Albion
The Hawthorns, Halford Lane (0121) 525 8888
Tickets from £15 (concessions £8.50)
Certainly the surprise package of the Nationwide Division One has been at The Hawthorns, where West Bromwich

Galaxy 102.2 THE NEW MIX FOR BIRMINGHAM

Albion have so far defied all odds and currently find themselves challenging for an automatic promotion place. The smallest and arguably the least commercially attractive of the three West Midlands clubs currently in the First Division, the Black Country side have demonstrated to their Wolverhampton neighbours the benefits of team spirit and cohesion above and beyond new stadiums and millions of pounds worth of talent. Presently clinging to the coat-tails of Birmingham City, the Baggies however are not short of skill and guile with the irrepressible Richard Sneekers and prolific Lee Hughes ensuring that for results and entertainment the Hawthorns is well worth a visit. Boing boing!

Wolverhampton Wanderers
Molineux Stadium, Waterloo Road (01902) 655 000

Tickets from £14 (concessions £9.50)
You've got the best stadium in the Midlands, a club superstore on site, a millionaire chairman, executive boxes, club restaurants, bars and a club with a strong and emotive past – what more could you want? Er, Premier League football?
Wolverhampton Wanderers have long been known as the First Division's perennial underachievers – declared bankrupt in 1982 and 1986 the club was rescued by the talismanic Sir Jack Hayward whose millions have been invested both on and off the field.
But, therein lies the problem – despite fantastic facilities and resources the Wolves have failed to mount a serious challenge to regain top flight status. Internal disputes

and rumours of financial ranglings have not helped the cause and unless there is a radical change of fortunes on the pitch the Wolverhampton faithful with have to contend themselves with a few more years in the First Division.

Birmingham Bullets Basketball Team
I.C.C Broad Street (0121) 246 6022
Adult £7.50

Twice Wembley Champions, the Bulletts are one team to keep your eye on. They've had a rollercoaster ride of ups and downs over the past season, with a new coach, owner and several new young players. Now in their 27th season they're looking to start European fixtures soon and with any luck, Birmingham will get to play host. For the latest on fixtures, check itchybirmingham.co.uk

Grand Prix Karting

Birmingham Wheels Karting Centre
Saltley (0121) 327 7617

Sat and Sun 10-1pm. Call ahead for times during the week.

Membership is free. You have to be 4ft 10ins tall.

£5 for 5 mins, £10 for 12 mins, £20 for 30 mins

Greyhound Racing at Hall Green Stadium

York Road (0121) 777 1181

Greyhound Racing at Perry Barr Stadium

Aldridge Road (0121) 356 2324

National Paintball Fields

Bassett's Pole, Sutton Coldfield
(0121) 327 3961

Sat and Sun 9.30-4.30pm

£39.50 Full day, includes lunch, equipment and 600 paintballs.

£55.50 Full day, includes lunch, equipment and 1000 paintballs.

£79.50 V.I.P. Full days, includes breakfast and lunch, tea/coffee all day, equipment and 1250 paintballs.

Students pay £10 and then £5 for every 100 paintballs.

When Gary from accounts gets right on your wick, it's time to take out your latent aggression by popping a cap in his ass.

Planet Ice

Pershore Street (0121) 693 2400

Ice skating session(s) 10-4pm, 7.30-10pm

Adults £4.50 to £6.00

NUS £2.00 on Student Night (Weds)

Warwickshire County Cricket

County Cricket Ground, Edgbaston
(0121) 446 4422

Tickets from £15

Scene of Brian Lara's historic innings of 501 n.o. against Durham in 1994, in a year which saw Warwickshire take home most of the silverware. Since then, legendary South African fast bowler Alan Donald has helped the side mount a serious challenge in the County Championship. In addition, successive Lords finals in trophy matches has demonstrated that the Bears are not a team to be taken lightly. This summer, the ground will be among the Test Match venues, as a revitalised England team take on Australia in the Ashes. It's worth a visit to watch some of the finest cricketers around, both at county and international level.

Casinos

China Palace Casino

Hurst Street (0121) 622 3313

great gaming

starts here

Restaurant & Bars
Open 7 Days a Week

2 casinos to choose from

For **FREE** membership call
FREEPHONE
08080 21 21 21

Birmingham
Walsall

Opening Times
2pm - 4am daily
6pm - 4am daily

Roulette Blackjack
Casino Stud Poker
Cardroom
Jackpot Machines

Please check individual casinos for gaming facilities

24 hours must elapse between receipt of application and participation in gaming.
Members must be aged 18 years and over.

Grosvenor Casino
Broad Street (0121) 631 2414

Ladbroke International Casino
Hill Street (0121) 643 1777

The Midland Wheel Casino
Norfolk Road, Edgbaston
(0121) 454 3725

Rainbow Casino
Portland Road, Edgbaston
(0121) 454 1033

| Strip Clubs

Exposé Lap Dancing Club
Fletchers Walk, Paradise Place
(0121) 236 5701
Admission £9 before 9pm and £10 afte
£5 a dance
Mon-Sat 8-3am

Legs 11
30 Ladywell Walk (0121) 666 7004

Legs 11 has now moved round the cor
ner, but the company has been going fo
longer than we can remember but the
idea is still the same. Remember that yes
she might be giving you the eye, and ye
she is absolutely starkers, but no, she isn'
interested and no she's not "mad for it"
Legs provides two floors and plenty of fi

and nubile girls in direct competition with Spearmint Rhino's.

Spearmint Rhino's
64 Hagley Road, Edgbaston
(0121) 455 7656
Admission £10
Mon-Wed 11am-2am, Thu-Sat 11am-3am, Sun 12-12am
The American chain has landed in the UK with this, their first venture, bringing a touch of class and sophistication to the often murky world of strip-joints. Sort of takes the fun out of it.

Zig Zag
Auchlinleck Square, Five Ways
(0121) 673 6743
More of the same. What else?

Bowling

Megabowl
Pershore Street (0121) 666 7525

Star City
Watson Road, Nechells (0121) 327 8483
Bowling doesn't get much bigger nor more American than this. With 22 lanes, glo-bowling Thu-Sat (lights go down to disco level and the luminous balls come out), a fully licensed bar, 12 American pool tables and a huge amusement arcade, you'd have thought they had the whole thing sewn up. But they've added a couple of dancefloors too; how's that for entertainment? Unpretentious, simple fun.

Snooker/Pool
See Star City above

Majestic Snooker Club
Station Street (0121) 632 6499

Rileys
Essex Street (0121) 666 6811

Snowhill Snooker Centre
Weaman Street (0121) 233 3953

Live Music Venues

The Birmingham Academy
Dale End, Priory Square 0870 903 2222
Possibly the best live music venue in Birmingham. With the paint still wet on the walls from its recent opening, the Academy, part of the same group that owns Shepherds Bush Empire and the Brixton Academy, promises to bring the best acts to the city. About bloody time too. For the latest listings, have a shoofty at itchybirmingham.co.uk. We'll be covering all the latest events in the city.

 **Galaxy 102.2** THE NEW MIX FOR BIRMINGHAM

The Fiddle & Bone

Sheepcote Street (0121) 200 2223

Jazz and blues, playing to an older crowd

Foundry

Beak Street (0121) 643 6843

Grunge, hardcore punk metal alternative motherf***kers. Full of anger and angst for the latest off-the-wall offerings from round the country.

The Jam House

St Paul's Square (0121) 200 3030

Another one for the older crowd – the place belongs to Jools Holland, so it should give you an inkling as to the musical style.

NEC

Jn 6 off M42 (the Coventry Rd, A45)
General enquiries 9-5 (0121) 767 3888

The busiest exhibition centre in Europe, with more than 180 exhibitions each year, from the International Motor Show to Crufts. Absolutely massive, attracting over 4 million people each year across 2 million square feet of exhibition space. Lots of trade fairs are held here, but from time to time there's various large-scale exhibitions such as the Ideal Home show which are worth a visit. As for the Arena, your best bet is to travel by car.

NEC Arena

As for NEC

From Pavarotti to Prince, if they're big (and brave) enough, you'll find them touring here. Sadly, this means the likes of those grinning gimps Westlife are just as likely to play here as the Rolling Stones but no matter. Bit of a trek out of town and best reached by car. Check itchybirmingham.co.uk for details.

NIA

King Edward Road 10-6pm 10-6pm
(0121) 644 6011

For The ICC, The NIA and Symphony Hall, call (0121) 644 6011 between 10am and 6pm.

Most famously host to Gladiators and some live music events – including All Saints. Shaznay playing Dual with Jet, the mind boggles. It's an impressively-sized venue, not quite as big as the NEC with 13,000 seats, but it's still big enough to host the World Indoor Athletics Championships (2003) and most importantly, the crooning of wannabes around our continent with the Eurovision Song Contest. Fantastic.

Ronnie Scott's Club
Broad Street (0121) 643 4525

Yet another for the older crowd (sense a trend here?), with jazz galore, and a healthy dollop of blues.

Symphony Hall
Broad Street (0121) 644 6011

One of the world's greatest concert halls, plays host to a variety of music, more in the Bach camp than big beat. Home to the City of Birmingham Symphony Orchestra with a variety of international and famous line-ups in the classical music world.

Birmingham Bus Tours
Birmingham Convention & Visitor Bureau, Colmore Row, Victoria Square (0121) 693 6300

May-Sept 10-4pm. Adults £8.00. NUS £6.50

A guided tour of the city from an open top bus. I'll be quite honest and tell you I've never been, but there's a good reason for that. Much as I love the city, lets face it, it's not Dublin is it?

Days Out/Attractions

Alton Towers
Stoke-on-Trent 0990 204060

Mar-Oct, Adults £21

21 quid gains you entrance to the UK's biggest and best rollercoasters and vertical-drop rides. The place holds no surprises but is consistently the best theme park in the country. Naturally quieter during the week without the hordes of schoolkids. A place for family and adults who aren't ready to grow up.

Black Country Museum
Tipton Road, Dudley (0121) 520 8054

Adults £7.95, NUS £4.75
Dec-Feb, Wed-Sun 10-4pm
Mar-Nov, Mon-Sun 10-5pm

The history of the Black Country (where 'yam yams' live, you know, the ones with the funny accent), all wrapped up in one open-air museum. There's lots of shops and re-created factories in their original form, complete with electric trams and out-of-work actors happily pretending they've never heard of the 20th Century. It could be tacky were it not for the fact it's on such an impressively large scale, that you can't fail to be sucked into this other world. Barge trips are particularly worth going on.

Cadbury World
Bournville Lane, Bournville
(0121) 451 4180
Adults £8.25, NUS £6.75
Reopening at the same time this book hits the shops, the new improved Cadbury World will appeal to chocolate-lovers and uh... well that's the whole point. It'll take you around two hours to go round the whole thing. It's a visitor centre, rather than a tour round the whole factory, and is best described as a slightly less glamourous version of Willie Wonka's Chocoloate Factory. There's a discount shop at the end of it, but don't expect any freebies.

Drayton Manor Family Theme Park
Nr Tamworth, Staffordshire
01827 287979
Mar-Oct. Adults £15
OK, not as good as Alton Towers, but then nothing else is in the UK. They've a couple of decent rides, including a stand-up rollercoaster called the Shockwave, shamelessly sponsored by an electricity company (and why not the hair product eh?). Best for kids and families.

Dudley Zoo & Castle
The Broadway, Dudley 01384 215313

Adults £6.50, NUS £4.50
10-5pm everyday (last admission 3pm)
50-acres of woodland and a spectacular array of beasties, from chimps to tigers. Not your usual pent-up dismal animals here – this place is big on conservation and protecting endangered species. No matter how old you are, I defy you to be impressed. The castle is inspiring too; a looming great creation from 1071. Next time you're hungover on a Sunday, give it a crack.

Lickey Hills
Visitor's Centre, Warren Lane, Barnt Green (0121) 447 1706
Acres of beautiful woodland and hills to stroll around. Two car parks, bracing winds and striking views.

National Sea Life Centre
The Water's Edge, Brindley Place
(0121) 633 4700
Adults £8.00, NUS £5.95
10-5pm (last admission 4pm)
Guaranteed to mess with your mind is the underwater tunnel where you'll be surrounded by sharks, rays and a load of other sealife which you'd be lucky to recognise, let alone name. Lots of impressive displays, marred only by a slightly educational feel to the place.

Stratford

William Shakespeare, bard and all-round top geezer hung out here in the 1500's, before popping off to London to get all theatrical. In fact if you can find something to do here that doesn't involve Bill you'll be doing well. Mind you, you'll be doing even better if you can avoid the combined populations of Chicago, Boston and Philadelphia, complaining about the food, wearing crap caps and mispronouncing Warwickshire. While you're there, you should really see ...

Shakespeare's Birthplace, Henley St – he was actually born here, no really, it's true.

River Avon – impromptu performances by random thesps, Bancroft Gardens, good for relaxing when you're all cultured out.

Shakespeare Centre – next door to the good man's birthplace. An exhibition of all things Shakespearian.

Anne Hathaway's Cottage, Shottery – a short walk out of town brings you to the one-time home of Shakespeare's wife. A beautiful, 15th century thatched farmhouse.

Warwick Castle
Warwickshire (01926) 406600
Adult £9.75 10-5pm

Seems like a lot of money for any castle, but at least it is genuinely grand and impressive. Occasionally, little men dress up and hit each other with swords recreating battles of old, though it's more Monkey Magic than Gladiator. Set aside at least a couple of hours to truly lap it up (mind you, at these prices, you're unlikely to do a supermarket dash).

West Midland Safari & Leisure Park
Spring Grove, Bewdley, Worcestershire (01299) 402114, Info (01299) 400700
Mar-Oct 10am last admission 3.30pm
Car – per person £5.95
Rides – Adult £7.00

Like Dudley, the rides are unlikely to thrill anyone except those devoid of intelligence (or age to be fair), but there's a hefty collection of tigers, giraffes and even hippopotami to make urban dwellers remember there's more to life than Spaghetti Junction. Laugh heartily as the wildlife rip the wing mirrors off your spanking new car.

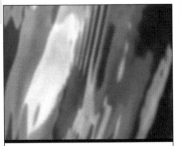

body

www.itchycity.co.uk

Curves & Co Birmingham
41 Smallbrook, Queensway
(0121) 643 8712

Large array of treadmill, rowing machines and other cardiovascular equipment. Services include specially tailored fitness programmes, dietary advice, aerobics classes and sauna. Rates from £3.45 per week.

LA Fitness
Unit 5, Temple Row (0121) 632 3950

Full range of the latest cardiovascular equipment made by Technogym, free weights, plus saunas, steams and a hydra pool (basically a playboy's Jacuzzi).
Monday- Friday 6am- 10pm, weekends 10am-6pm

LivingWell Health Club
3 Brunswick Arcade, Brindley Place
(0121) 633 4645

Open week days 6.30am-10.30pm weekends 10am-7pm. Membership £49 per month (Gold membership) £39 pe month (Casual membership).

LivingWell Health & Leisure
42-44 The Priory Queensway
(0121) 236 7789
Open week days 6.30am-10.30pm,
weekends 10am-7pm. Membership £49
per month (Gold membership) £39 per
month (Casual membership).

Moseley School Health & Fitness Centre
College Road, Moseley (0121) 678 1290

Physique Fitness Studio
103A High Street, Harborne
(0121) 428 3947

Planet Fitness
73-75 Pershore Street (0121) 693 2405

Ralph's Gym & Fitness
Lordswood Road, Harborne
(0121) 426 5066

Temple Gym
6 Temple Pass, Temple Street
(0121) 643 7964

Leisure Centres

Aston Villa Sports & Leisure Centre
Aston Hall Road (0121) 464 8330
Open Monday-Friday 10am-11pm,
Closed Saturday. Sunday 10am-9pm.

Birmingham Sports Centre
201 Balsall Heath Road, Highgate
(0121) 678 1120

Gilletts Sports Centre
998 Bristol Rd, S. Oak (0121) 415 2300

Snowdome Ski & Snowboarding Centre
Leisure Island, River Drive, Tamworth
(01827) 67905
Monday-Friday £10 for your first hour
before 6.15pm, £15 after. Weekends
£19 for your first hour, £13 members.

Tudor Grange
Blossomfield Road, Solihull
(0121) 711 1628
Mon, Thu, Fri 8.30-8pm, Tue, 8.30-7.30
Wed 8.30-7.45pm (adults 8-9), Sat 9.30-
5, Sun 8-5.30
Swimming pool from £1.75, Paradise
Falls £3 unlimited use wristband

Aside from being a whopping great swimming pool with diving boards, this place is home to Paradise Falls. The Bahamas it isn't, but there are three big waterslides, including one near vertical drop, not for the faint-hearted or those who mind getting their keks in a twist.

Hair – Women

Bliss
13 Edgbaston Shopping Centre
Hagley Road
(0121) 624 6241
Monday- Friday 9.30am-6pm, Thursday 10am-7pm, Saturday 9.30am-5pm. Cuts start from £12.50.

Carnaby Cutting Room
648 Pershore Road, Selly Oak
(0121) 471 3777

Copperfields
319 Harborne Lane, Harborne
(0121) 471 2933

Hair City One
6 The Big Peg, Warstone Lane, Jewellery Quarter (0121) 236 8081

Harborne Hair Studio
433 Court Oak (0121) 427 8877

Reflections
163 High Street, Harborne
(0121) 427 2411

Rimski Hair
852 Bristol Road, Selly Oak
(0121) 472 0445

Hair – Men

Azura
489 Bristol Road, Selly Oak
(0121) 472 6289
9am-5.30pm Monday-Saturday Cuts from £7

City Clippers
137 School Road, Moseley
(0121) 444 1088
Monday-Friday 9am-6pm Saturday 8am-4pm. Cuts from £8

Headman
788 Bristol Road, Selly Oak
(0121) 471 1888
Mon- Wed 10am-5.30pm, Thu & Fri 10am-6pm, Sat 10am-5pm. Cuts from £5.50

Michael's
451 Brook Lane (0121) 624 6222

Hair – Unisex

Boo
43 Stephenson Street (0121) 632 5949
Monday- Friday 9.45am-6pm, Saturday 8am-6pm. Cuts from £23.50

www.itchybirmingham.co.uk

Eden

11 Ethel Street (0121) 633 3834
Monday - Friday 10am-5pm, Saturday
9am-3pm Cuts from £26

N19

19 Temple Street (0121) 643 1919

Phase 2

591 Bristol Road South (0121) 475 4329
Monday-Friday 9am-5, Thursdays 9am-
3pm, Saturdays 8.30am-5pm. Cuts from
£10.90

Toni + Guy

Cannon Street (0121) 631 3333
9.30am-6pm, Thursday 9.30am-6.30pm,
Saturday 9am-3pm. Cuts from £23

Umberto Giannini

**The Water Edge, Brindley Place
(0121) 633 0111**
Monday-Wednesday 10am-7pm,
Thursday & Friday 10am-8pm, Saturday
8.30am- 5pm. Cuts £18-£37.50

And you are? Will, 20, Student
For a few sharpeners? Stoodi Bakers – if
you can bare the noise
Best night in town? Code Red at Code
For somewhere to eat? Any balti house,
any where, any time
Best shop? Cult Clothing
Brum, what's good? It's cheaper than
London, loads to do with cracking clubs
What's not? Waiting for the redevelop-
ment to finish

Beauty

Health & Hair Clinic
234 Soho Road (0121) 551 7503

The Body Shop
New Street (0121) 233 1239

Clarins Studio
Corporation Street (0121) 212 2336

LUSH
31 Corporation Street (0121) 643 2700

Tranquilo The Beauty Centre
**3rd Floor Guildhall Building, Navigation
Street (0121) 687 7717**
Beautiful staff and beautiful customers to
make you feel gorgeous.

body

takeaway

www.itchycity.co.uk

Chicken

Fiesta Southern Fried Chicken
37 Constitution Hill
(0121) 236 1228

Bull Ring Chick King
39-40 Bull Ring (0121) 643 1460

The Fried Dumpling
41 Bull Ring (0121) 643 0341

Asian

Dewan Tandoori Take Away
216 St. Vincent Street West
(0121) 456 4972

Star Tandoori
212 Monument Road (0121) 455 661

Burgers & kebabs

Dins Kebab House
178 Corporation Street
(0121) 212 9488

Mr Egg
22 Hurst Street (0121) 622 4344
An institution in Birmingham. Who else
would have the cheek to call themselves
something so off-puttingly minging as Mr
Egg and yet still do a roaring trade?

City Kebab House
29 Constitution Hill (0121) 236 9991

Kayas Turkish Take Away
Sound people, great food, cheap and lot
of kebabs.

Pizza

Pizza & Pasta
Kiosk 5 Food Court, Pavilions

Caspian Pizza
23 Smallbrook Queensway
(0121) 643 7882
Pizza / Vegiburgers, delivered and t/way

Sicilian Dial-A-Pizza
161 Hagley Road (0121) 456 4322

Prago Pizza
163 Hagley Road (0121) 455 9916

Chinese

Ivy House Chinese Take Away
213 Monument Road (0121) 454 4215

Jumbo House
214 St Vincent Street (0121) 454 7737

Sum Ye Chinese Fast Food
Unit 105, Arcadian Centre
Lightening-quick service and tasty, best
said in a Glaswegian accent.

Yeungs Restaurant
Unit 2 Kotwell House, Ladywell Walk

Sandwiches

Coffee Republic
82-3 New Street (0121) 633 8310

Dunkin Donuts
82-83 New Street (0121) 643 9465
Unit 2 Great Western Arcade
(0121) 233 9729
Kiosk 19 Bridge Link, Bull Ring Centre

Pret-A-Manger Europe Ltd
22 Colmore Row (0121) 236 4616
52 New Street (0121) 633 3637
Paradise Forum, Paradise Place

Subway Sandwiches
85 Bull Street (0121) 212 9019

Philpotts Quality Sandwiches
141 Great Charles Street, Queensway
31 Edgbaston Shopping Centre
(0121) 452 1024
Best sandwiches in Brum, guaranteed.

  Find your nearest takeaway on your phone
wap.itchybirmingham.co.uk

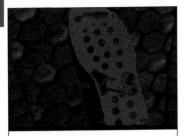

getting
about

www.itchycity.co.uk

Bus and local rail

Centro is responsible for Birmingham's public transport system, and as much as you can complain, they're doing as much as they can given the fact that Birmingham was never built to accommodate such tremendous amount of traffic.

Bus/local rail   (0121) 200 2700

Coaches

Digbeth coach station, perhaps the grottiest station in the whole country, at the hub of major coach routes

National Express   0990 808080

Planes

Birmingham International Airport is the gateway to Europe and rest of the world. It's around 15 minutes from Birmingham on the A45 (signposted off the M40 and M6).

Flight enquries   (0121) 767 7798/9
Airport info desk (0121) 767 7798/9
Car parking   (0121) 767 7831
Car parking (long)   0800 128128

Trains

Birmingham New Street is right in the heart of the city centre with easy access to taxis and buses. There's all kind of redevelopment going on, but you can still reach it by car if you follow the diversion signs carefully. Moor Street and Snow Hill stations are both decent commuter centres as well, with easy access to the centre of the city.

National rail enquiries 0345 484950 (24 hour service).
Virgin trains   (0121) 654 9400

British Rail International (European
destinations)   (020) 7834 2345
Eurostar   0345 303030

Tourist

Stratford Tourist Information
Centre   (01789) 293127

Warwick Tourist Information
Centre   (01926) 492212

B'ham Convention
& Visitor Bureau   (0121) 780 4321

Hospitals

Birmingham Childrens Hospital
(0121) 454 4851

Birmingham Dental Hospital
(0121) 236 8611

Birmingham Heartlands Hospital
(0121) 608 6688

Birmingham Nuffield Hospital
(0121) 456 2000

City Hospital
(0121) 554 3801

Priory Hospital
(0121) 440 2323

Queen Elizabeth Hospital
(0121) 472 1311

Selly Oak Hospital
(0121) 627 8226

Taxis – central

T.O.A. Taxis
(0121) 426 4588 / 236 8888 / 427 8888
Birmingham Falcon Cars
                        (0121) 233 0000
Elmdon Cars   (0121) 780 2222
Bell Cabs Black Cabs
                        (0121) 782 1122.
Airshuttle Mini Coach Service
                        (0121) 558 4163
5 Ways Cars   (0121) 455 8181 /
      456 4499 / 454 1994 / 454 5165
B.B's Taxis
            (0121) 693 3333 / 233 3030
Victoria Cars   (0121) 554 0304

Taxis – Moseley, Harborne, Selly Oak

Royal Cars   (0121) 444 8888
Central Line   (0121) 233 3344
Quinbourne   (0121) 604 5000

Rental cars (all central)

Thrifty   (0121) 327 8515
Avis Rent a Car   (0121) 632 4361
Enterprise Rent-a-Car
                        (0121) 643 7743
Budget   (0121) 643 0493
Hertz   (0121) 643 5387
Europcar   (0121) 622 5311

Universities

Aston switchboard (0121) 359 6531
Aston Guild   (0121) 359 3611
B'ham switchboard (0121) 414 3344
B'ham Guild   (0121) 472 1841
UCE switchboard   (0121) 331 5000
UCE Guild   (0121) 331 6801

getting about

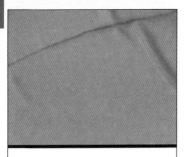

accommodation

www.itchycity.co.uk

We've given the cheapest rooms available here – usually at weekend tariff. During the week and in peak season, it can be loads more expensive (up to 50%), so ring first before you get too excited...

Comfort Inn
Station Street (0121) 643 1134
Single starting from: £55 inc. breakfast

Burlington Hotel
New Street (0121) 643 9191
Single starting from: £70 inc. breakfast
The most classically swanky hotel in Birmingham. Sartorial elegance abounds.

Copthorne Hotel
Paradise Circus (0121) 200 2727
Single starting from: £140 room only

Hyatt Regency
2 Bridge Street (0121) 643 1234
Single starting from: £85 room only
Modern and plush hotel catering to the wealthy end of the business market.

Novotel

Broad Street (0121) 643 2000
Single starting from: £70 inc. breakfast

Crowne Plaza

Central Square (0121) 631 2000
Single starting from: £68 inc. breakfast

Forte Travelodge

Broad Street (0845) 740 4040
Single room starting from: £49 room only

Chamberlain Tower Hotel

Broad Street (0121) 626 0626
Single starting from: £55 inc. breakfast

Hagley Road is excellent for cheaper accommodation, varying from standard hotels to B&Bs – if these are full up, there are plenty more down this road. It's a short hop from the city centre in a cab.

Apollo

243 Hagley Road (0121) 455 0271
Single starting from: £45 room only. Location for 'In the Name of the Father' (ie. it's still authentically 70s)

Plough & Harrow

135 Hagley Road (0121) 454 4111
Single starting from: £45 inc. breakfast

Quality Cobden Hotel

166/174 Hagley Road (0121) 454 6621
Single starting from: £39 inc. breakfast

Woodlands Hotel

379 Hagley Road (0121) 420 2341
Single starting from: £35 inc. breakfast

▌ B&Bs

Belmont Hotel

419 Hagley Road (0121) 429 1663
Single starting from: £18 inc. breakfast

Cook House Hotel

Hagley Road (0121) 429 1916
Single starting from: £20 inc. breakfast

Hamilton House

290 Hagley Road (0121) 429 9849
Single starting from: £15 room only. Excellent value friendly B & B

Victoria Halls

17 Grange Road, Selly Oak
(0121) 256 7000. www.victoriahall.com
If you are a student or have been a student then you will appreciate that words "luxury" and "student housing" don't sit together comfortably. Student houses should come with a government health warning (at least the ones I've stayed in). At Victoria Hall however, you'll find brand spanking new student housing. Fully furnished flats and each room with their own shower and toilet; Sky TV in each flat, a telephone, 24-hour manned security and CCTV, and a fully-equipped kitchen. Despite being within pint spilling distance of one of the best pubs in Sellyoak, there's precious few reasons for students to step outside their own front door. These houses are a good deal better than the places I've lived in even since finishing Uni, and more to the point you won't be afraid to show it to your parents. They even have a 24-hour Tesco just down the road – you lucky studes.

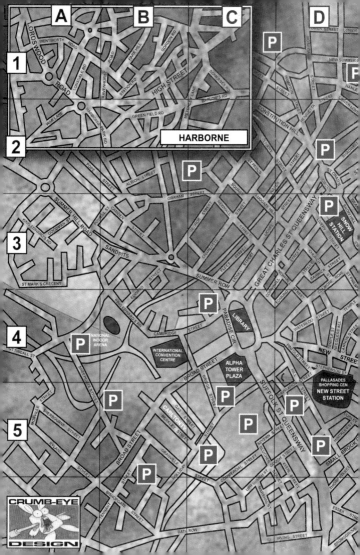

index

120

www.itchybirmingham.co.uk